SKINNY COOKING

Skinny Italian

COOKING

◆——————◆

RUTH GLICK
NANCY BAGGETT

SURREY BOOKS

CHICAGO

SKINNY ITALIAN COOKING is published by Surrey Books, Inc.
230 E. Ohio St., Suite 120, Chicago, IL 60611.

First edition: 1 2 3 4 5

This book is manufactured in the United States of America.

Library of Congress Cataloging-in-Publication data:

Glick, Ruth.
    Skinny Italian cooking / by Ruth Glick and Nancy Baggett.—1st. ed.
    207p. cm.
    Includes index.
    ISBN 0-940625-98-9 (pbk.)
    1. Cookery, Italian. 2. Low-fat diet—Recipes. 3. Salt-free diet—
Recipes. 4. Low-calorie diet—Recipes. I. Baggett, Nancy, 1943– . II. Title.
TX723.G625 1996
641.5'63'0945—dc20   96-1578
                                           CIP

Editorial and production: *Bookcrafters, Inc., Chicago*
Art Director: *Joan Sommers Design, Chicago*
Cover and interior illustrations by *Mona Daly*

For free catalog and prices on quantity purchases, contact Surrey Books at the
address above.

This title is distributed to the trade by Publishers Group West.

Titles in the "Skinny" Cookbooks Series:

Skinny Beef	*Skinny Pasta*
Skinny Chicken	*Skinny Pizzas*
Skinny Chocolate	*Skinny Potatoes*
Skinny Comfort Foods	*Skinny Sandwiches*
Skinny Desserts	*Skinny Sauces & Marinades*
Skinny Grilling	*Skinny Seafood*
Skinny Italian Cooking	*Skinny Soups*
Skinny Mexican Cooking	*Skinny Spices*
Skinny One-Pot Meals	*Skinny Vegetarian Entrées*

CONTENTS

FULL-FLAVOR, LOWER-FAT RECIPES

Italian cooking, with its rich tradition of regional specialties and simple classics, is one of the great cuisines of the world. It's also an American favorite. Witness the popularity of pastas and pizzas in their infinite variety; thick, hearty soups like minestrone; and that darling of the dessert cart, tiramisu.

Italian cooks had a head start on culinary sophistication. Roman citizens were dining at opulent banquets when most of the world's inhabitants were still charring antelope over open fires. And the great city-states of the Renaissance were as famous for their dining pleasures as their art treasures.

Down through the centuries, Italian fare has come to rely on a variety of flavorful ingredients: herbs like oregano, thyme, basil, rosemary, garlic, and parsley; cheeses such as Parmesan, mozzarella, and ricotta; and fruits of the land, including tomatoes, sweet peppers, and olives with their wonderfully aromatic oil. A number of these products, like olives, basil, and thyme, were native to the Mediterranean region. Others, like tomatoes, potatoes, bell peppers, and corn, came from the New World but over time were incorporated into Italian cuisine.

Perhaps as a result of ready access to fine cheeses and quality olive oil, many traditional Italian recipes weigh in on the high end of the fat and calorie scales. Today, despite our continuing love affair with Italian cuisine, most Americans want lighter, less calorie-laden meals. Is it possible to slim down Italian food and still enjoy the authentic taste of Mamma Luisa's specialties?

Happily, the answer is yes. During the 15 years we've been designing better-for-you recipes, we've found that moderation is the key to successfully creating rich-tasting, satisfying, low-fat fare. Practically speaking, while it doesn't usually work to remove every smidgeon of fat, we can definitely cut back on it without sacrificing great taste. A little fat can go a long, long way—particularly when we take other steps to compensate for the increased leanness of a recipe.

In certain dishes we have subtly shifted the balance of ingredients. Less of the high-fat elements are used while some very flavorful lower-fat ones—like herbs and spices, wine, chicken broth, and tomatoes—play a slightly more prominent role. Often, we have also substituted leaner cuts of meat and poultry for fattier ones and have taken advantage of reduced-fat ingredients available on American supermarket shelves—for instance, low-fat and nonfat cheeses. These lend the expected full flavor and impart a sense of richness yet still trim back on fat.

Fortunately, we have been able to assign pasta its usual starring role because this foundation food of Italian cuisine is naturally lean. Most brands of dry pasta have less than 2 grams of fat (about $1/2$ teaspoon) per 4-ounce plateful. Even fresh, refrigerator-case pastas, which may have 4 to 8 grams of fat per generous portion (often due to the inclusion of egg yolks), are still fat "bargains" relative to many prepared foods. As for calories, pasta, pizza doughs, and similar lean carbohydrate foods have only 4 per gram while oil and other fats have 9 calories per gram. Recent claims suggesting a link between pasta and weight gain have been discounted by most experts, who say that fats, not pastas, are usually the cause.

Though our primary emphasis in *Skinny Italian Cooking* has been reducing fat (and trimming sodium) to make dishes more healthful, the recipes also have been modified to fit into today's busy lifestyles. The majority of dishes can be prepared in 45 minutes and a number in far less time. Some recipes suggest using convenience products such as prepared pasta sauce or frozen vegetable mixtures so you can get a home-cooked dinner on the table in a snap. And we include microwaving time-savers and food processor shortcuts throughout.

FULL-FLAVOR, LOWER-FAT RECIPES

vii

Skinny Italian Cooking covers a whole range of wonderful foods—
from classics like Pepperoni Pizza, Chicken Cacciatore, and Spaghetti with
Meat Sauce to regional specialties such as Tuscan Bean Soup, Focaccia
with Onions and Sun-Dried Tomatoes, and Risotto and Peas. Nor do we
skimp on desserts. There's a chapter full of sweet treats, ranging from
Chocolate-Hazelnut Biscotti and Zuppa Inglese to Tiramisu and Lemon
Granita. With this collection, you can quickly and easily bring the vibrant,
flavorful cookery of Italy to your table, yet simultaneously avoid excess fat
and calories. Enjoy!

A Skinny
Cooking Primer

Skinny Italian Cooking is more than a collection of Italian favorites
updated for today's lighter tastes. It's also an excellent guide to low-
fat cooking methods and ingredients. Simply by using the recipes,
you'll discover a lot about creating healthful yet delicious meals.

All of the techniques in this book are easy, although some may be a
little different from what you're used to. For example, to reduce the
amount of fat needed to saute without burning, some recipes call for combining olive oil with a small amount of broth or wine. Others call for trimming meat or skimming fat from the tops of soups, stews, and sauces with
a large, shallow spoon. These are simple steps, yet very effective in reducing excess fat.

Equipment

Luckily, there's not much specialized equipment needed for low-fat cooking. About the only essential is a nonstick skillet. (Actually, it's handy to have several in different sizes. We each own 12-inch and 10-inch nonstick skillets, plus other shapes such as deep-sided Dutch oven/saute combo pans.) If you're considering new cookware, look for brands that feature the most modern and improved nonstick finishes, which hold up better and require less tender care than earlier coatings.

A number of our recipes also utilize the microwave oven either for all or part of the cooking. One obvious reason is that microwaving can reduce cooking time. In addition, vegetables such as onions, garlic, and mushrooms can be "sauteed" in the microwave with no fat added. Dishes like risotto and polenta are easier to make in the microwave oven because far less stirring than normal is required.

All microwave recipes in this book were tested in 900-watt units. If you have one with a different rating, you may need to adjust cooking times.

Ingredients

We've been asked which low-fat ingredients we regularly substitute for higher fat ones. Actually, there's no magic formula for creating great-tasting food with less fat. What tastes wonderful in one recipe may be a complete bust in another. One of the reasons we test all of our recipes extensively is to discover which alternative works best in each situation.

Here are some of the ingredients we've used frequently in *Skinny Italian Cooking*:

Olive Oil. Although the rich, fruity taste of olive oil is an important flavor component in Italian cooking, most traditional recipes use far more than is actually needed. We've cut considerable fat by trimming back the oil and then boosting the quantity of onions, garlic, and other aromatic ingredients to preserve fine flavor. Except when cooking at a very high temperature, we usually prefer to use extra-virgin olive oil because it has the fullest flavor.

Cheese. In Italian classics from pizza to eggplant Parmesan, cheeses figure prominently. But since cheese is high in fat, we use a number of sneaky techniques—like substituting lower-fat versions or cutting back the overall amount. For example, if a recipe calls for slices of mozzarella, we switch to shredded, which can go farther. Also, we sometimes get maximum impact by sprinkling cheese over a dish rather than mixing it in. Incidentally, there are a number of reduced-fat cheeses on the market. We like the taste of some much better than others, so experiment to decide which you prefer.

Parmesan, especially fresh-grated, is a wonderful flavor booster because it has an intense, distinctive taste and a little goes a long way. And it's also relatively low in fat. An ounce of grated Parmesan (¼ cup) has only 7 grams of fat. We call for it in a number of recipes. However, in some dishes we've found that grated nonfat Parmesan topping is also acceptable, and it saves even more fat. In some recipes we effectively combine the two.

Mozzarella cheese is another frequent component of Italian cooking, and one with a considerable amount of fat. As a result, some recipes call for part-skim mozzarella, with about 5 grams of fat per ounce, or the reduced-fat variety, with 3.5 grams of fat per ounce. For even greater savings, we occasionally stretch these with some nonfat mozzarella.

In many dishes nonfat ricotta works well, and the fat and calorie savings are dramatic. However, in some recipes part-skim ricotta does yield better results.

In several desserts and appetizers we use Neufchâtel, a part-skim cream cheese which has one-third the fat of regular cream cheese. Occasionally, Neufchâtel and nonfat cream cheese are combined.

Eggs and Egg Substitutes. All of the fat in an egg is in the yolk. So in most recipes that call for eggs, we either eliminate the yolks or use more whites than yolks. Some recipes need a few yolks for flavor. However, in most standard baked goods that call for eggs, it works perfectly well to use one white in place of each whole egg. In a few recipes we also call for liquid egg substitute, which is made from whites. Most brands have no fat, but check labels to be sure.

Reduced-Fat Mayonnaise. This is now common on supermarket shelves. However, there is a confusing assortment of products to choose from—some with no fat, others with varying amounts. In this book we call for mayonnaise with 5 grams of fat per tablespoon because we think it's the best tasting alternative to the full-fat kind.

Meats. People often think that cutting dietary fat means going meatless. We can assure you it doesn't! Check the nutritional information provided with our recipes, and you'll see that the fat content of our meat dishes is often lower than in traditional vegetarian fare. One way we accomplish this is by calling for the lowest-fat cuts—ground round, round steak, flank steak, pork tenderloin, chicken breast, and turkey breast. Also, in a number of recipes that are traditionally made with veal (such as classic veal marsala and country-style veal stew) we've substituted far leaner turkey breast, with truly delicious results.

We've also found that stretching ground beef with ground turkey breast is a great way to cut fat in meatballs and meat sauces. To retain a robust beefy taste and to ensure that the poultry blends in completely, we always use more ground beef than ground turkey in the mixtures.

Note that our recipes call for ground turkey breast, not ground turkey, which can be as high in fat as ground beef. More and more supermarkets sell ready-to-use ground turkey breast meat, or they will grind fresh boneless turkey breasts or cutlets for customers on request. Where this service isn't available, it's a simple matter to grind cut-up breast meat at home using the food processor. Then the meat can be divided into smaller portions and frozen for later use.

Another of our fat-trimming techniques is to use a small amount of a very flavorful meat to season a large quantity of sauce. For example, some recipes call for ham, bulk sausage, or pepperoni but use them judiciously and/or rely on reduced-fat or very lean versions of products.

Broth. Particularly, fat-free chicken broth plays an important role in a number of our recipes. Sometimes it helps to keep vegetables from burning during "sauteing." Sometimes it can substitute for part of the oil in salad dressings and marinades. Several brands of fat-free broth are available, but you can also defat broth yourself simply by using a shallow spoon and skimming fat from the surface.

Wine. The fruity, full-bodied flavor and acidity of wine enlivens and enriches a number of classic Italian meat and poultry dishes and has the advantage of adding no fat.

On occasion, we call for dry red or white wine, as well as for marsala and sherry. Unless we specify a particular type, any pleasant dry table wine or sherry will do, although an Italian variety will lend an authentic touch. In some cases we indicate that an alcohol-free wine may be used. On the other hand, cooking wine or sherry is not satisfactory due to its high salt content.

Vinegars and Lemon Juice. These ingredients are also important in skinny Italian recipes. With their pungent aroma and penetrating taste, they tingle the tastebuds and perk up the flavor of slimmed-down fare. For best results, use the type of vinegar specified, such as red wine or balsamic, and use fresh lemon juice if it's called for.

Herbs. Probably the most frequently employed herbs in Italian cooking are oregano, basil, thyme, garlic, rosemary, parsley, chives, and sage—all of which are used liberally in *Skinny Italian Cooking.* Most recipes call for dried herbs, although in some cases fresh is best. That is always true of parsley since it loses virtually all of its taste during drying. We also prefer fresh chives and suggest substituting green onions when they are not available. For convenience in a number of recipes, we call for a commercial "Italian seasoning" blend, which combines thyme, basil, oregano, and rosemary.

Nutritional Analysis

The only way to appreciate the richness and flavor of these reduced-fat recipes is to cook them. But you can judge their healthfulness by the nutritional information that follows each one. The analysis, done by a registered dietitian using the latest professional computer software, although not infallible, tells how many calories and how much fat, saturated fat, cholesterol, protein, carbohydrate, and sodium are in each serving. Diabetic exchanges are also provided for those who might find them useful.

Remember that many factors can affect the accuracy of nutritional data: variability in sizes of fruits, vegetables, and other foods; variability in weights and measures of foods; a possible plus or minus of 20 percent error factor in labeling of prepared foods; and variations in personal cooking methods.

Sodium is also kept to a minimum in these recipes. With some products, we call for a reduced-sodium alternative first but give you the option of using the regular one if that's what you have on hand. In most recipes we also suggest how much salt to add but make this optional for those restricting sodium intake.

Where the recipe gives a choice of ingredients or range of quantities, the nutritional analysis is always based on the first alternative. Optional and "to taste" ingredients are not included in the analyses, nor are garnishes.

If you have any health problems that require strict dietary requirements, it is important to consult a physician, dietitian, or nutritionist before using these recipes or those found in any other cookbook.

About the Recipes

All of our recipes are tested at least three times and often more to make sure directions are easy to follow and proportions are correct. We have emphasized readily available ingredients and usually suggest alternatives for those that may be hard to find. Convenience items are suggested or used when we feel they significantly shorten preparation time and still yield tasty results.

1
ANTIPASTI

Hot Artichoke Spread

Caponata with Crostini

Sun-Dried Tomatoes and Peppers Spread

Chick Pea Spread

Crostini with Tomato and Basil

Pizza Rollups

Olive Flatbread Crisps

HOT ARTICHOKE SPREAD

A subtle blend of taste and texture, this artichoke spread is won-
derfully rich and creamy. The mayonnaise used in the recipe has
5 grams of fat per tablespoon because we find it tastes better
than lower-fat ones yet it still significantly lightens recipes. We
like serving this spread on toasted Italian bread, but nonfat or
reduced-fat crackers also work well.

Makes 1³/₄ cups (25 servings)

 1 14–15-oz. jar water-packed artichoke heart
 quarters, rinsed and well drained
 ¹/₃ cup (1¹/₂ ozs.) grated Parmesan cheese
 ¹/₃ cup nonfat sour cream
 ¹/₄ cup Neufchâtel cream cheese
 ¹/₄ cup reduced-fat mayonnaise (5 grams of fat
 per tablespoon)
 1 small garlic clove, minced
 3–4 drops hot pepper sauce
 ¹/₄ cup chopped chives, *or* very thinly sliced green
 onion tops
 1 large loaf Italian bread, cut into serving-sized
 slices and toasted

1. Remove and discard tough outer leaves of artichoke hearts. Coarsely
   chop hearts. Set aside in a small bowl.
2. In a medium-sized bowl, combine Parmesan cheese, sour cream,
   Neufchâtel cheese, mayonnaise, garlic, and hot pepper sauce. Stir with
   a spoon until well blended. Add chives and reserved artichokes. Stir to
   mix well.
3. Transfer mixture to a small glass or ceramic microwave-proof casserole or bowl. Cover with casserole lid or wax paper, and microwave on
   high power 3 to 4 minutes or until heated through; turn the casserole
   ¹/₄ turn once during microwaving. Serve hot.

Nutritional Data

PER SERVING		EXCHANGES	
Calories:	80	Milk:	0.0
% Calories from fat:	27	Vegetable:	1.0
Fat (gm):	2.4	Fruit:	0.0
Sat. fat (gm):	0.9	Bread:	0.5
Cholesterol (mg):	3.4	Meat:	0.0
Sodium (mg):	173	Fat:	0.5
Protein (gm):	3.1		
Carbohydrate (gm):	11.9		

CAPONATA WITH CROSTINI

◆

Even people who don't care for eggplant often enjoy the spicy spread called caponata. Served with crostini, toasty-crisp slices of Italian bread, it makes a tempting—and surprisingly satisfying—low-fat appetizer. Traditional caponata recipes call for baking the eggplants, which takes nearly an hour. Here, we ready them in a microwave oven in about 15 minutes.

25 Servings

2 medium-sized eggplants, about 1 pound each
2 tablespoons olive oil, preferably extra-virgin, divided
2 large onions, chopped
2 large garlic cloves, minced
1 cup finely diced red bell pepper
2 medium-sized fully ripe tomatoes, peeled and chopped
1½ tablespoons pitted, finely chopped oil-cured black olives, *or* kalamata black olives
½ teaspoon granulated sugar
⅛ teaspoon black pepper
Pinch of hot red pepper flakes
2–3 teaspoons lemon juice, to taste
¼–½ teaspoon salt (optional)
1 large loaf Italian bread

1. *For caponata:* Pierce eggplants several times all the way through using a sharp, thin knife. Place an eggplant on a microwave-proof plate. Microwave on high power 6 to 9 minutes or until eggplant is soft, stopping and turning over after 4 minutes. Repeat with second eggplant. Set aside until cool enough to handle.

2. Meanwhile, in a 12-inch nonstick skillet over medium-high heat, combine 1 tablespoon oil, onions, garlic, and peppers. Adjust heat so vegetables gently cook. Saute, stirring occasionally, about 10 minutes or until onions are golden. Stir in tomatoes, olives, sugar, pepper, and red pepper flakes.

3. Adjust heat so mixture simmers briskly. Cook, uncovered and stirring occasionally, 10 minutes.

4. Meanwhile, cut open the eggplants. Scrape eggplant pulp into a colander. Press down on pulp to extract as much liquid as possible. Add pulp to skillet. Continue simmering about 25 minutes longer until mixture has cooked down and flavors are well blended. Add lemon juice and salt to taste. Spread may be made ahead and stored, refrigerated, 3 or 4 days. Let warm to room temperature before serving.

1. *For crostini:* Shortly before serving time, preheat oven to 325 degrees. Cut bread crosswise into scant 1/2-inch-thick slices. Brush one side of slices very lightly with remaining olive oil. Cut slices in half. Lay slices on large baking sheet. Toast 10 to 15 minutes until slices are lightly browned, turning once. Cool slightly and serve with the caponata.

Nutritional Data

PER SERVING		EXCHANGES	
Calories:	80	Milk:	0.0
% Calories from fat:	23	Vegetable:	1.0
Fat (gm):	2.1	Fruit:	0.0
Sat. fat (gm):	0.3	Bread:	0.5
Cholesterol (mg):	0	Meat:	0.0
Sodium (mg):	125	Fat:	0.5
Protein (gm):	2.3		
Carbohydrate (gm):	13.9		

SUN-DRIED TOMATOES AND PEPPERS SPREAD

*Here, simple ingredients produce a rich and flavorful spread.
The secret is in cooking the vegetable mixture until the
peppers are very tender.*

Makes 3 cups (24 servings)

- 3/4 cup dry-packed sun-dried tomatoes
- 1 16-oz. bag red, green, and yellow frozen bell peppers and onions
- 1 tablespoon olive oil
- 2 garlic cloves, minced
- 2 teaspoons Italian seasoning
- 1/2 teaspoon salt, *or* more to taste (optional)
- 1/8 teaspoon black pepper
- 1/2 cup shredded reduced-fat mozzarella cheese
- 1 loaf Italian bread cut into serving-sized slices and toasted, *or* nonfat crackers

1. In a small bowl, cover tomatoes with hot water. Let stand 5 to 10 minutes to soften. Drain and chop. Cut up any large pieces of onion in the peppers-onions mixture.

2. In a 12-inch nonstick skillet, combine peppers and onions mixture, reserved tomatoes, oil, garlic, Italian seasoning, salt, if desired, and black pepper. Stir to mix well. Cook uncovered over medium heat 10 to 15 minutes, stirring frequently, or until onions and peppers are tender. Remove from heat. Transfer to a shallow bowl. Stir in cheese.

3. Serve warm with Italian bread or nonfat crackers.

Nutritional Data

PER SERVING		EXCHANGES	
Calories:	72	Milk:	0.0
% Calories from fat:	20	Vegetable:	1.0
Fat (gm):	1.6	Fruit:	0.0
Sat. fat (gm):	0.3	Bread:	0.5
Cholesterol (mg):	0	Meat:	0.0
Sodium (mg):	162	Fat:	0.0
Protein (gm):	2.3		
Carbohydrate (gm):	12.3		

CHICK PEA SPREAD

Chick peas have been featured prominently in Italian cuisine since ancient times. Here, we've used them in a tasty spread. Serve it as an appetizer or a snack.

Makes 1¹/₂ cups (33 servings)

¹/₃ cup boiling water
¹/₄ cup quartered dry-packed sun-dried tomatoes
1 15-oz. can chick peas, washed and drained
1 garlic clove, minced
1 tablespoon olive oil
1 tablespoon lemon juice
¹/₄ cup chopped chives, *or* green onion tops
1 teaspoon dried thyme leaves
¹/₂ teaspoon dried basil leaves
¹/₄ teaspoon (scant) salt (optional)
¹/₈ teaspoon black pepper
  Nonfat crackers, *or* Italian bread

1. In a small bowl, combine water and tomatoes. Allow tomatoes to soften for about 10 minutes. Transfer tomatoes and water to a food processor container. Add chick peas, garlic, oil, and lemon juice. Process until chick peas are smooth and tomatoes are in very small pieces. Transfer to medium-sized bowl.

2. Stir in chives, thyme, basil, salt, if desired, and pepper. If spread seems stiff, add a bit more water. Cover and refrigerate 2 or 3 hours or up to 24 hours before serving.

3. Serve on nonfat crackers or Italian bread.

Nutritional Data

PER SERVING		EXCHANGES	
Calories:	42	Milk:	0.0
% Calories from fat:	15	Vegetable:	0.0
Fat (gm):	0.7	Fruit:	0.0
Sat. fat (gm):	0.1	Bread:	0.5
Cholesterol (mg):	0	Meat:	0.0
Sodium (mg):	114	Fat:	0.0
Protein (gm):	1.5		
Carbohydrate (gm):	7.3		

CROSTINI WITH TOMATO AND BASIL

Here's a marvelous technique for flavoring oven-crisped bread, or crostini, without adding tons of fat. Topped with tomato and basil, this savory bread is a great appetizer. Or skip the tomato and basil topping, and serve along with the meal as a wonderful, reduced-fat substitute for garlic bread.

12 Servings

- 1 13-oz. loaf unsliced Italian bread
- 1/2 cup fat-free, reduced-sodium chicken, *or* vegetable broth
- 1/2 cup grated nonfat Parmesan cheese topping
- 2 tablespoons olive oil
- 1 tablespoon red wine vinegar
- 2 garlic cloves, minced
- 1/2 teaspoon dried thyme leaves
- 1/8 teaspoon salt (optional)
- 1/8 teaspoon black pepper
- 2 medium-sized tomatoes, cut into 1/4-in. slices
  Additional salt (optional)
- 12 fresh basil leaves

1. Preheat oven to 350 degrees. Discard heels of bread. Cut remainder of bread into 3/4-inch slices. Arrange bread on a large, rimmed baking sheet. Set aside.

2. In a 2-cup measure, combine broth, cheese, oil, vinegar, garlic, thyme, salt, if desired, and pepper. Whisk until smooth. Spoon mixture evenly over bread slices, spreading it with back of spoon.

3. Bake in preheated oven 20 minutes or until bread begins to brown. Top each bread slice with a tomato slice. Sprinkle lightly with salt, if desired. Add a basil leaf to each. Serve immediately.

Nutritional Data

PER SERVING		EXCHANGES	
Calories:	127	Milk:	0.0
% Calories from fat:	27	Vegetable:	1.0
Fat (gm):	3.9	Fruit:	0.0
Sat. fat (gm):	0.9	Bread:	1.0
Cholesterol (mg):	1.1	Meat:	0.0
Sodium (mg):	256	Fat:	0.5
Protein (gm):	4.7		
Carbohydrate (gm):	18.6		

PIZZA ROLLUPS

———◆———

This easy recipe turns ordinary pizza into a crowd-pleasing appetizer. It's best made with our Basic Pizza Crust, page 156. However, for convenience, you could substitute pizza dough from the dairy case. If you like, the rollups can be served with extra pizza sauce for dipping.

16 Servings

1 rectangular pizza crust, approximately 11 in. x 14 in. (see Basic Pizza Crust recipe, page 156)

1/2 cup reduced-fat, reduced-sodium pizza sauce, *or* regular pizza sauce

2 ozs. (1/2 cup loosely packed) shredded reduced-fat mozzarella cheese

2 ozs. (1/2 cup loosely packed) shredded nonfat mozzarella cheese

1/4 cup grated nonfat Parmesan cheese topping, divided

Extra pizza sauce for dipping (optional)

1. Preheat oven to 375 degrees. Place crust on a large nonstick baking sheet coated with cooking spray. Spoon sauce onto crust, and spread it out evenly. Sprinkle mozzarella cheeses evenly over sauce. Sprinkle with Parmesan, reserving 1 tablespoon for topping.

2. Roll pizza from long end as if for a jellyroll. Cut roll in half to form two rolls. Turn rolls seam-side down. With fingers, stretch out each roll evenly along its length to form two 11 to 12-inch rolls, being careful not to tear dough and keeping rolls as round as possible. (If dough tears, some filling may leak out during baking, but this will not affect the appearance of the rolls when they are cut and served.)

3. Bake 15 to 18 minutes or until rolls are lightly browned on top. (Baking time may be slightly shorter if a purchased crust is used.) Remove from oven. Cool slightly. With a sharp knife, cut off ends of rolls and discard. Cut into 1-inch slices and arrange on a serving plate. Sprinkle pinwheels with remaining Parmesan. Serve hot. If desired, provide extra pizza sauce for dipping.

Nutritional Data

PER SERVING		EXCHANGES	
Calories:	81	Milk:	0.0
% Calories from fat:	16	Vegetable:	0.0
Fat (gm):	1.4	Fruit:	0.0
Sat. fat (gm):	0.3	Bread:	1.0
Cholesterol (mg):	0	Meat:	0.0
Sodium (mg):	147	Fat:	0.0
Protein (gm):	3.9		
Carbohydrate (gm):	13		

OLIVE FLATBREAD CRISPS

*Served warm from the oven, these simple, chewy-crisp flatbread
wedges make wonderfully savory, munchable hors d'oeuvres.
The olives add just the right zip, so the wedges need no spread
or dip. We've found that it is worth seeking out top-quality
Italian or Greek cracked green olives—they have a richer,
fuller flavor than less expensive salad olives.*

*Although the crisps are best when very fresh, for convenience,
they may be transferred to an oven-proof serving platter;
covered with foil; and then rewarmed in a 375-degree oven
for 10 to 12 minutes before serving.*

Makes 24 crisps (1 per serving)

2¼–2½ cups all-purpose white flour, divided
1 packet fast-rising dry yeast
¾ cup water
1½ tablespoons extra-virgin olive oil, divided
¾ teaspoon salt
½ cup chopped, pitted cracked green olives,
preferably Italian or Greek
1 tablespoon grated Parmesan cheese

1. Combine 1¼ cups white flour and yeast in a food processor fitted with a steel blade. Pulse several times to mix well.

2. Combine water, 1 tablespoon oil, and salt in a saucepan. Stirring until salt dissolves, heat mixture over medium-high heat to 125 degrees (or until it feels hot but does not burn fingertips).

3. With processor running, pour liquid through feed tube into flour mixture until all has been added. Process 1½ minutes. Add 1 cup more flour. Process until flour is incorporated; if dough does not form a firm ball that cleans the container sides, gradually add more flour until it reaches that point.

4. Transfer dough to a medium-sized nonstick, spray-coated bowl. Lightly brush top of dough with a small amount of remaining olive oil. Cover bowl with plastic wrap. Set aside in a warm place to rise, about 25 minutes. Meanwhile, coat a 12-inch-round pizza pan with nonstick spray.

5. Preheat oven to 475 degrees. Working in bowl, punch down dough. Pat and press olives between paper towels until dry. Sprinkle dough with olives; knead until incorporated. On a lightly-floured work surface, press and shape dough into a round by hand or with a rolling pin. Place on pizza pan. Brush dough with remaining olive oil.

6. Bake in upper third of oven 12 to 16 minutes or until round is nicely browned and slightly puffed. Remove from oven. Slide round onto a cutting board. Using pizza wheel or sharp knife, cut round into quarters. Cut each quarter into 6 wedges. Return wedges to pizza pan. Sprinkle with Parmesan cheese. Return to oven and bake 2 or 3 minutes longer until Parmesan melts. Serve immediately, or reheat to warm at serving time.

Nutritional Data

PER CRISP		EXCHANGES	
Calories:	56	Milk:	0.0
% Calories from fat:	23	Vegetable:	0.0
Fat (gm):	1.4	Fruit:	0.0
Sat. fat (gm):	0.2	Bread:	0.5
Cholesterol (mg):	0.2	Meat:	0.0
Sodium (mg):	145	Fat:	0.5
Protein (gm):	1.5		
Carbohydrate (gm):	9.1		

2
SALADS

Penne Salad with Artichokes

Italian Garden Orzo Salad

Binnie's Pasta Salad

Tuna-Pasta Salad

Rice Salad

Potato and Green Bean Salad

Bread Salad

Lentil Salad

PENNE SALAD WITH ARTICHOKES

To easily turn this into a main-dish salad, substitute a cup of cooked cannellini beans for one cup of the pasta.

7 Servings

Dressing

- 1/2 cup fat-free reduced-sodium chicken broth, *or* vegetable broth
- 1/4 cup fresh lemon juice
- 1/2 cup chopped fresh parsley leaves
- 3 tablespoons diced oil-packed sun-dried tomatoes
- 3 tablespoons olive oil, preferably extra-virgin
- 2 tablespoons freshly grated Parmesan cheese
- 3 tablespoons chopped fresh basil leaves, *or* 1 teaspoon dried basil leaves
- 1 1/4 teaspoons dried marjoram leaves
- 1/4 teaspoon each: black pepper and salt

Salad

- 6 cups cooked and cooled penne (about 10 1/2 ozs. uncooked)
- 1 14-oz. jar water-packed artichoke hearts, well-drained, tough leaves removed, hearts quartered
- 2/3 cup chopped red bell peppers
- 1/4 cup coarsely chopped green onions, *or* finely chopped fresh chives
- 2 large, ripe tomatoes, coarsely diced

1. *For dressing:* In a large nonreactive bowl, mix broth, lemon juice, parsley, sun-dried tomatoes, oil, Parmesan, basil, marjoram, pepper, and salt until well blended. Let stand a few minutes so flavors can blend.

2. *For salad:* Thoroughly combine penne, artichoke pieces, peppers, and green onions. Add dressing; stir until ingredients are thoroughly mixed. Refrigerate at least 30 minutes and up to 24 hours, if desired. Toss with tomatoes at serving time.

Nutritional Data

PER SERVING		EXCHANGES	
Calories:	279	Milk:	0.0
% Calories from fat:	25	Vegetable:	2.5
Fat (gm):	7.8	Fruit:	0.0
Sat. fat (gm):	1.3	Bread:	2.0
Cholesterol (mg):	1.4	Meat:	0.0
Sodium (mg):	202	Fat:	1.5
Protein (gm):	9.6		
Carbohydrate (gm):	44.7		

ITALIAN GARDEN ORZO SALAD

Colorful, fresh tasting, and easy, this makes a nice addition to a buffet or picnic. It can be prepared a day ahead, if desired.

7 Servings

1¼ cups (about 8 ozs.) uncooked orzo
1 cup each: diced carrots and celery
1 cup each: diced red and yellow bell peppers
⅓ cup chopped green onions, *or* finely chopped fresh chives
¼ cup plus 1 tablespoon fresh lemon juice
½ cup chopped fresh parsley leaves
2½ tablespoons olive oil, preferably extra-virgin
½ teaspoon dried marjoram leaves
½ teaspoon finely grated lemon zest (yellow part of peel)
¼ teaspoon each: black pepper and salt
Romaine leaves or other crisp lettuce leaves, for garnish

1. Cook orzo according to package directions until just *al dente*. Turn out into a colander. Rinse under cold water; drain well.

2. In a large serving bowl, stir together carrots, celery, red and yellow peppers, and green onions.

3. In a small nonreactive bowl, mix lemon juice, parsley, oil, marjoram, lemon zest, pepper, and salt until well blended. Pour mixture over diced vegetables.

4. Add orzo to vegetables, tossing until thoroughly blended. Refrigerate at least 30 minutes and up to 24 hours, if desired. Serve salad on romaine leaves, if desired.

Nutritional Data

PER SERVING		EXCHANGES	
Calories:	200	Milk:	0.0
% Calories from fat:	25	Vegetable:	0.5
Fat (gm):	5.7	Fruit:	0.0
Sat. fat (gm):	0.7	Bread:	2.0
Cholesterol (mg):	0	Meat:	0.0
Sodium (mg):	100	Fat:	1.0
Protein (gm):	5.5		
Carbohydrate (gm):	32.9		

BINNIE'S PASTA SALAD

This tangy pasta salad is adapted from a recipe given to us by a very dear friend. If summer tomatoes are unavailable, substitute 5 or 6 Italian plum tomatoes.

7 Servings

Dressing

- 2½ tablespoons red wine vinegar
- 2 tablespoons tomato paste
- 1 tablespoon water
- 2 tablespoons granulated sugar
- 2 tablespoons olive oil
- 1 garlic clove, minced
- ¼ teaspoon dried oregano leaves
- ¼ teaspoon dried basil leaves

Salad

- 1 cup uncooked elbow macaroni
- 1 cucumber, peeled, halved, seeded, and chopped
- 1 large tomato, cubed
- ¼ cup chopped chives, *or* sliced green onion tops
- 1 medium-sized green or red bell pepper, seeded and chopped
- 1 cup broccoli florets

1. *For dressing:* In a serving bowl, combine vinegar, tomato paste, and water. Stir to mix well. Stir in sugar, oil, garlic, oregano, and basil. Set aside.

2. *For salad:* Cook macaroni according to package directions. Transfer to a colander and rinse under cold running water. Drain.

3. Meanwhile, add cucumber, tomatoes, chives, peppers, and broccoli to bowl with dressing. Stir to mix well. Stir in macaroni. Refrigerate 1 hour or up to 36 hours before serving. Stir before serving.

Nutritional Data

PER SERVING		EXCHANGES	
Calories:	124	Milk:	0.0
% Calories from fat:	30	Vegetable:	0.5
Fat (gm):	4.3	Fruit:	0.0
Sat. fat (gm):	0.6	Bread:	1.0
Cholesterol (mg):	0	Meat:	0.0
Sodium (mg):	44	Fat:	1.0
Protein (gm):	3.1		
Carbohydrate (gm):	19.5		

TUNA-PASTA SALAD

For a pleasant change from traditional American tuna salad,
try this version with artichoke hearts and pasta.

5 Servings (main dish)

1 10-oz. package frozen artichoke hearts, *or* 1, 12–14-oz. can artichoke hearts

1/3 cup fat-free reduced-sodium chicken broth, *or* vegetable broth

1/4 cup grated nonfat Parmesan cheese topping

2 tablespoons olive oil

1 tablespoon red wine vinegar

1 tablespoon Italian seasoning

1/4 teaspoon salt (optional)

1/8 teaspoon black pepper

1½ cups uncooked fusilli, cooked according to package directions, rinsed and drained

5 Italian plum tomatoes, cut into bite-sized pieces

1/4 cup thinly sliced green onion tops

1 large red, green, or yellow bell pepper, seeded and cubed

1 6-oz. can water-packed white tuna, drained

1. Pull off and discard tough outer leaves from artichoke hearts. If using frozen ones, cook according to package directions and cool in a colander under cold water. If using canned, drain in colander. Cut hearts into small wedges. Set aside.

2. In a large bowl, combine broth, cheese, oil, vinegar, Italian seasoning, salt, if desired, and black pepper. Stir to mix well.

3. Add fusilli, reserved artichoke hearts, tomatoes, green onions, and peppers. Stir to mix well. Fold in tuna. Serve immediately at room temperature, or refrigerate several hours or up to 24 hours before serving.

Nutritional Data

PER SERVING		EXCHANGES	
Calories:	333	Milk:	0.0
% Calories from fat:	21	Vegetable:	4.0
Fat (gm):	8	Fruit:	0.0
Sat. fat (gm):	1.3	Bread:	1.5
Cholesterol (mg):	14	Meat:	1.5
Sodium (mg):	298	Fat:	1.0
Protein (gm):	21.6		
Carbohydrate (gm):	48.2		

RICE SALAD

◆

*This hearty salad comes from a wonderful little restaurant
in the Italian hill town of San Gimignano. Although it was served
as an accompaniment to our main dish, we also like to showcase
it as a lunch or summer supper entree.*

6 Servings (side dish)

1 cup uncooked long-grain white rice
1/4 cup fat-free, reduced-sodium chicken broth, *or*
    regular defatted chicken broth
1 tablespoon olive oil
1 tablespoon red wine vinegar
2 teaspoons Italian seasoning
1/4 teaspoon salt (optional)
1/8 teaspoon black pepper
1 large red or yellow bell pepper, seeded and
    cubed
1 cup shredded cabbage
1/4 cup minced chives, *or* thinly-sliced green
    onion tops
1 oz. pitted black olives (about 5 large), sliced
4 ozs. fully cooked turkey sausage, diced

1. Cook rice according to package directions.

2. While rice is cooking, in a large serving bowl, combine broth, oil,
    vinegar, Italian seasoning, salt, if desired, and black pepper. Stir to
    mix well. Stir in bell peppers, cabbage, chives, and olives. Set aside.

3. Meanwhile, in a medium-sized nonstick skillet, cook sausage over
    medium heat until it is heated through and begins to brown, 2 or 3
    minutes. Stir sausage into vegetable mixture. Add rice to bowl, and
    stir to mix well. Serve warm, or cover and refrigerate several hours
    or up to 24 hours. Stir before serving.

Nutritional Data

PER SERVING		EXCHANGES	
Calories:	189	Milk:	0.0
% Calories from fat:	30	Vegetable:	1.0
Fat (gm):	6.4	Fruit:	0.0
Sat. fat (gm):	0.9	Bread:	1.5
Cholesterol (mg):	15.3	Meat:	0.0
Sodium (mg):	166	Fat:	1.0
Protein (gm):	5.8		
Carbohydrate (gm):	27.1		

POTATO AND GREEN BEAN SALAD

Tarragon vinegar sets off the flavors of the potatoes and green beans in this zesty salad.

Don't overcook the potatoes. If left slightly firm, they hold together when stirred into the dressing and also do not absorb as much liquid (and fat) as well-done potatoes.

6 Servings

    1 lb. green beans, trimmed and snapped in half
1¹/₂ lbs. red-skinned potatoes, cut into ³/₄-in. cubes (4 cups)
    3 tablespoons fat-free, reduced-sodium chicken broth, *or* vegetable broth
    2 tablespoons olive oil
    2 teaspoons tarragon vinegar
  ¹/₄ cup chopped chives, *or* thinly sliced green onion tops
  ³/₄ teaspoon tarragon leaves
  ¹/₂ teaspoon Dijon-style mustard
  ¹/₄ teaspoon salt, *or* to taste (optional)
      Pinch of ground white pepper

1. Combine green beans and enough water to cover in a medium-sized saucepan. Cover and bring to a boil. Lower heat and boil 10 to 15 minutes or until just tender. Transfer to colander and cool slightly under cold running water. Drain well.

2. Meanwhile, combine potatoes and enough water to cover in a separate large saucepan. Cover and bring to a boil. Reduce heat and simmer 10 to 13 minutes or until potatoes are tender but do not break apart when pierced with a fork. When potatoes are cooked, transfer them to a colander and cool slightly under cold running water. Then drain well.

3. While vegetables are cooking, in a large bowl or serving dish, combine broth, oil, and vinegar. Stir to mix. Add chives, tarragon, mustard, salt, if desired, and pepper. Stir to mix well.

4. Add vegetables, carefully stirring with a large spoon to coat with dressing mixture. Be careful not to break up the potatoes. Cover and refrigerate several hours, stirring occasionally, to allow flavors to blend.

Nutritional Data

PER SERVING		EXCHANGES	
Calories:	148	Milk:	0.0
% Calories from fat:	28	Vegetable:	1.0
Fat (gm):	4.8	Fruit:	0.0
Sat. fat (gm):	0.7	Bread:	1.0
Cholesterol (mg):	0	Meat:	0.0
Sodium (mg):	30	Fat:	1.0
Protein (gm):	3		
Carbohydrate (gm):	25.1		

BREAD SALAD

◆

*We were introduced to this unusual salad at one of
New York's most exclusive Italian restaurants and loved
the concept since the crunchy bread cubes make such a nice
contrast to the crisp greens. To keep the bread crisp, be sure
to dry the romaine well after rinsing it.*

6 Servings

Dressing
<ul style="list-style:none">
<li>1/2 cup fat-free, reduced-sodium chicken broth, or vegetable broth</li>
<li>1/4 cup grated nonfat Parmesan cheese topping</li>
<li>1 1/2 tablespoons olive oil</li>
<li>1 tablespoon red wine vinegar</li>
<li>1/4 teaspoon salt (optional)</li>
<li>1/8 teaspoon black pepper</li>
</ul>

Salad
<ul style="list-style:none">
<li>7–8 large romaine lettuce leaves, torn into pieces (about 10 cups)</li>
<li>2 large tomatoes, cubed</li>
<li>1 medium cucumber, peeled, seeded, and cubed</li>
<li>1/4 cup thinly sliced chives, or green onion tops</li>
<li>1/4 cup chopped fresh basil leaves, or 1 teaspoon dried basil leaves</li>
<li>5 cups (5 ozs.) 1-in. bread cubes made from stale Italian bread (if unavailable, toast fresh bread slightly)</li>
</ul>

1. *For dressing:* In a 2-cup measure or similar deep bowl, whisk together broth, Parmesan, oil, vinegar, salt, if desired, and pepper. Whisk to mix well. Set dressing aside.

2. *For salad:* Rinse romaine and dry well with paper towels or tea towel. In a large salad bowl, mix together romaine, tomatoes, cucumbers, chives, and fresh basil. (If using dried basil, mix it into the salad dressing in Step 1.)

3. Pour dressing over salad, and toss to mix. Lightly toss in bread cubes. Serve at once. Alternatively, to prepare salad 6 to 8 hours ahead, make dressing and refrigerate. Prepare salad ingredients and transfer to

serving bowl. Prepare bread and store in a plastic bag. Just before serving, assemble salad.

Nutritional Data

PER SERVING		EXCHANGES	
Calories:	139	Milk:	0.0
% Calories from fat:	30	Vegetable:	1.0
Fat (gm):	4.8	Fruit:	0.0
Sat. fat (gm):	0.7	Bread:	1.0
Cholesterol (mg):	0	Meat:	0.0
Sodium (mg):	199	Fat:	1.0
Protein (gm):	6.1		
Carbohydrate (gm):	19.4		

LENTIL SALAD

◆

*Serve this hearty salad as a side dish or as a summer
vegetarian main dish. The cooking time of the lentils will
vary according to their age and degree of doneness you prefer.
Be sure to cook the lentils in a large pot as they tend to foam
up and boil over in a small one.*

6 Servings

1½ cups uncooked green or brown lentils, washed
   and picked over
1 garlic clove, minced
1 large bay leaf
1 15-oz. can reduced-sodium tomato sauce, *or*
   regular tomato sauce
2 tablespoons olive oil
1 tablespoon lemon juice
1 tablespoon Dijon-style mustard
2 teaspoons dried oregano leaves
1¼ teaspoons dried thyme leaves
¼ teaspoon salt, *or* to taste (optional)
⅛ teaspoon black pepper
1 medium-sized zucchini, diced
½ large red bell pepper, seeded and chopped
¼ cup thinly sliced green onion tops, *or* chopped
   chives

1. In a 5-quart or larger pot, combine lentils, garlic, and bay leaf. Cover and bring to a boil. Reduce heat and simmer 30 to 40 minutes or until lentils are tender.

2. Meanwhile, in a large bowl, combine tomato sauce, oil, lemon juice, mustard, oregano, thyme, salt, if desired, and black pepper. Stir to mix well. Stir in zucchini, bell peppers, and onions.

3. Transfer lentils to a colander. Drain well. Stir into tomato sauce and vegetables mixture. Allow to stand 10 minutes so flavors can blend. Serve warm or chill up to 24 hours before serving. Garnish with chopped parsley, if desired.

Nutritional Data

PER SERVING		EXCHANGES	
Calories:	229	Milk:	0.0
% Calories from fat:	20	Vegetable:	1.0
Fat (gm):	5.3	Fruit:	0.0
Sat. fat (gm):	0.7	Bread:	2.0
Cholesterol (mg):	0	Meat:	0.0
Sodium (mg):	58	Fat:	1.0
Protein (gm):	13.3		
Carbohydrate (gm):	33.9		

3
SOUPS

Chick Pea and Pasta Minestrone

Hearty Minestrone with Pepperoni

Tortellini Soup

Italian Bread Soup

Tuscan Bean Soup

Bean and Spinach Soup Pronto

Potato and Onion Soup

Easy Venetian Fish Soup

Chicken-Vegetable Soup with Endive

CHICK PEA AND PASTA MINESTRONE

Try this interesting minestrone variation. Substantial and wonderfully flavorful, it's a snap to make. If you don't have the leftover ham called for, you can use Canadian bacon.

7 Servings

1 large onion, chopped
2 large carrots, peeled and thinly sliced
2 large celery stalks, thinly sliced
2 cups chopped cabbage
2 garlic cloves, minced
6 cups fat-free, reduced-sodium chicken broth, *or* regular defatted chicken broth
1 15-oz. can chick peas, rinsed and drained
1 14½-oz. can reduced-sodium Italian-style tomatoes, *or* regular tomatoes
1 medium-sized pork hock (about 10 ozs.)
4–5 ozs. leftover reduced-sodium ham, cut into small pieces
1 tablespoon Italian seasoning
⅛ teaspoon black pepper
½ cup (3 ozs.) uncooked orzo

1. In a Dutch oven or similar heavy pot, combine onions, carrots, celery, cabbage, garlic, broth, and chick peas. Add tomatoes, breaking them up with a spoon. Add pork hock, ham, Italian seasoning, and pepper. Cover and simmer 30 to 35 minutes, stirring occasionally until flavors are well blended.

2. Meanwhile, cook pasta according to package directions. Rinse and drain well in a colander. Add pasta to the soup, and simmer an additional 2 or 3 minutes. Remove and discard pork hocks. With a large, shallow spoon, skim and discard any fat from top of soup.

Nutritional Data

PER SERVING		EXCHANGES	
Calories:	191	Milk:	0.0
% Calories from fat:	13	Vegetable:	2.0
Fat (gm):	2.9	Fruit:	0.0
Sat. fat (gm):	0.5	Bread:	1.5
Cholesterol (mg):	3.7	Meat:	0.5
Sodium (mg):	684	Fat:	0.0
Protein (gm):	11.5		
Carbohydrate (gm):	31		

HEARTY MINESTRONE WITH PEPPERONI

◆

Pepperoni is very fatty, but since it's also quite flavorful, a little goes a long way in this full-bodied soup. Serve along with crusty bread and a salad for an easy, satisfying supper.

5 Servings (main dish)

1 tablespoon olive oil, preferably extra-virgin, divided

1 large onion, chopped

1 large celery stalk, coarsely diced

2 medium-sized carrots, coarsely diced

3/4 cup coarsely diced red bell pepper

2 large garlic cloves, minced

1/4 cup finely diced pepperoni, *or* hard salami

3 1/2 cups fat-free, reduced-sodium chicken broth, *or* regular defatted chicken broth

2 cups water

2 1/2 teaspoons dried basil leaves

1 teaspoon dried marjoram leaves

1/2 teaspoon dried oregano leaves

1/4 teaspoon black pepper, *or* to taste

Pinch of hot red pepper flakes (optional)

1/2 cup uncooked small macaroni

2 medium-sized zucchini, coarsely diced

1 28-oz. can reduced-sodium Italian-style tomatoes, including juice, chopped, *or* regular Italian-style tomatoes, including juice

1 19-oz. can cannellini beans, *or* Great Northern
   white beans, rinsed and well drained
   Salt to taste (optional)

1. In a 6-quart or similar large pot, heat oil to hot, but not smoking, over
   high heat. Add onions, celery, carrots, bell peppers, and garlic. Cook,
   stirring, 4 minutes. Add pepperoni; cook 4 or 5 minutes longer or until
   onion is browned.

2. Add broth, water, basil, marjoram, oregano, black pepper, and pepper
   flakes, if desired. Bring mixture to a boil, stirring occasionally. Lower
   heat; simmer, covered, 15 minutes.

3. Bring mixture to a rolling boil. Stir in macaroni and zucchini. When
   mixture returns to a boil, lower heat to simmer. Cook 8 to 10 minutes
   or until macaroni is almost tender.

4. Stir in tomatoes and their juice and beans. Simmer a few minutes
   longer until vegetables are tender and flavors are well blended. Add
   salt, if using.

Nutritional Data

PER SERVING		EXCHANGES	
Calories:	265	Milk:	0.0
% Calories from fat:	20	Vegetable:	3.0
Fat (gm):	6.9	Fruit:	0.0
Sat. fat (gm):	1.4	Bread:	2.0
Cholesterol (mg):	0	Meat:	0.5
Sodium (mg):	603	Fat:	0.5
Protein (gm):	17		
Carbohydrate (gm):	45.1		

TORTELLINI SOUP

◆

We rely on ready-to-use tortellini from the dairy case for this flavorful and speedy soup, which makes a nice luncheon or light supper entree.

4 Servings

2 teaspoons olive oil
1 large onion, chopped
1 garlic clove, minced
3 tablespoons dry sherry, *or* white wine
1 cup finely chopped parsley leaves
4½ cups fat-free, reduced-sodium chicken broth, *or* regular defatted chicken broth
1 9-oz. package reduced-fat cheese-and-garlic tortellini
2 teaspoons Italian seasoning
⅛ teaspoon black pepper, *or* to taste
1 15-oz. can reduced-sodium tomato sauce, *or* regular tomato sauce
1 teaspoon granulated sugar (optional)

1. In a Dutch oven or similar large pot, combine oil, onions, garlic, and sherry. Cook 5 or 6 minutes until onions are softened. Stir in parsley. Cook an additional 1 or 2 minutes.

2. Add broth, tortellini, Italian seasoning, and pepper. Cover and bring to a boil. Reduce heat and simmer 9 to 10 minutes or until tortellini are almost tender. Add tomato sauce. Stir to mix well. Bring to a boil, cover, reduce heat and simmer 12 to 15 minutes or until flavors are blended. Taste soup. If tomato seems acid, add sugar.

Nutritional Data

PER SERVING		EXCHANGES	
Calories:	298	Milk:	0.0
% Calories from fat:	16	Vegetable:	3.0
Fat (gm):	5.5	Fruit:	0.0
Sat. fat (gm):	1.9	Bread:	2.0
Cholesterol (mg):	33.7	Meat:	1.0
Sodium (mg):	659	Fat:	0.5
Protein (gm):	17.3		
Carbohydrate (gm):	46.2		

ITALIAN BREAD SOUP

*Although this delicious recipe comes from very humble origins,
we first encountered it in a trendy Italian restaurant in
Washington, D.C. The soup is a subtle blend of many tastes
and textures, but we've simplified the preparation. Note
that we've substituted seasoned crouton stuffing mix for
the traditional stale bread. (Check the labels on crouton stuffing
packages since they vary considerably in fat content.)*

8 Servings

    1 large onion, chopped
    1 large garlic clove, minced
    2 teaspoons olive oil
    6 cups fat-free, reduced-sodium chicken broth,
       or regular defatted chicken broth, divided
    1 15-oz. can reduced-sodium tomato sauce, *or*
       regular tomato sauce
    2 large carrots, peeled and chopped
    1 19-oz. can cannellini beans, rinsed and drained
    1 16-oz. bag frozen mixed broccoli, corn, and red
       bell peppers
 1½ cups chopped cabbage
    1 teaspoon each: Italian seasoning and dried
       basil leaves
  ¼ teaspoon black pepper
    2 cups low-fat seasoned crouton (cube-style)
       stuffing mix
       Salt to taste (optional)

1. In a Dutch oven or similar large, heavy pot, combine onions, garlic, oil, and 3 tablespoons broth. Cook over medium heat, stirring occasionally, until onions are tender, 5 or 6 minutes.

2. Add remaining broth, tomato sauce, carrots, beans, frozen vegetables, cabbage, Italian seasoning, basil, and black pepper. Bring to a boil. Cover, reduce heat, and simmer 30 minutes, stirring occasionally. Add salt if desired.

3. For each serving, place ¼ cup stuffing mix in a soup bowl; add soup.

Nutritional Data

PER SERVING		EXCHANGES	
Calories:	178	Milk:	0.0
% Calories from fat:	9	Vegetable:	3.0
Fat (gm):	2.1	Fruit:	0.0
Sat. fat (gm):	0.2	Bread:	1.0
Cholesterol (mg):	0	Meat:	0.0
Sodium (mg):	529	Fat:	0.5
Protein (gm):	12.5		
Carbohydrate (gm):	33.9		

TUSCAN BEAN SOUP

The Tuscans love beans. This wonderful, robust soup is just one of the reasons why!

6 Servings

- 2 cups dried cannellini, *or* Great Northern, beans
- 2 tablespoons olive oil, preferably extra-virgin
- 1 large onion, chopped
- 3 medium-sized carrots, diced
- 2 large garlic cloves, minced
- 1½ cups diced lean, well-trimmed ham
- 3 cups fat-free, reduced-sodium chicken broth, *or* regular defatted chicken broth, divided
- ½ teaspoon each: dried thyme leaves and dried marjoram leaves
- ½ teaspoon dried finely crumbled rosemary
- ⅛ teaspoon each: black pepper and dried hot red pepper flakes
- 1 cup diced reduced-sodium Italian-style canned tomatoes, including juice, *or* regular Italian-style tomatoes, including juice
- ¼ teaspoon salt (optional)

1. In a large soup pot, combine beans with 2 quarts water. Bring to a boil. Adjust heat so mixture boils gently and cook, covered, 1 hour. Drain beans into a colander. Wash out pot.

2. Combine oil, onions, carrots, and garlic in pot previously used. Cook over medium-high heat 6 or 7 minutes or until onions are lightly browned. Add ham; cook 2 minutes longer. Stir in 2 cups broth, thyme, marjoram, rosemary, black pepper, and red pepper flakes.

3. Combine 1½ cups beans with remaining 1 cup broth in a food processor or blender. Process or blend until pureed. Stir into vegetable-broth mixture, along with remaining beans.

4. Return mixture to a boil. Adjust heat so soup simmers gently. Cook, covered, stirring frequently to be sure beans are not sticking, until beans are completely tender, 35 to 45 minutes longer. Add tomatoes and juice; cook 10 minutes longer until flavors are blended. Add salt, if desired. Thin soup with more broth or water, if necessary.

Nutritional Data

PER SERVING		EXCHANGES	
Calories:	265	Milk:	0.0
% Calories from fat:	22	Vegetable:	2.0
Fat (gm):	6.7	Fruit:	0.0
Sat. fat (gm):	1.3	Bread:	2.0
Cholesterol (mg):	8.5	Meat:	1.0
Sodium (mg):	511	Fat:	0.5
Protein (gm):	19.3		
Carbohydrate (gm):	33.8		

BEAN AND SPINACH SOUP PRONTO

Beans and spinach are a classic Italian combination—
which we've used together in this hearty soup.

7 Servings (main dish)

6 cups fat-free, reduced-sodium chicken broth,
   or regular defatted chicken broth
½ cup uncooked orzo
6 ozs. Canadian bacon, cut into thin slivers
1 tablespoon Italian seasoning
1 garlic clove, minced
⅛ teaspoon black pepper
1 15-oz. can reduced-sodium tomato sauce, *or*
   regular tomato sauce
1 19-oz. can cannellini beans, undrained
1 10-oz. package frozen chopped spinach,
   thawed but not drained
   Salt to taste (optional)

1. In a large, heavy pot, bring broth to a boil. Add orzo, bacon, Italian seasoning, garlic, and pepper. Cook, uncovered, 11 to 12 minutes or until orzo is tender.

2. Add tomato sauce, beans, and spinach. Return to a boil, reduce heat, and simmer, covered, an additional 15 minutes. Add salt if desired.

Nutritional Data

PER SERVING		EXCHANGES	
Calories:	211	Milk:	0.0
% Calories from fat:	10	Vegetable:	2.0
Fat (gm):	2.6	Fruit:	0.0
Sat. fat (gm):	0.6	Bread:	1.5
Cholesterol (mg):	11.6	Meat:	1.0
Sodium (mg):	802	Fat:	0.0
Protein (gm):	18.8		
Carbohydrate (gm):	34.1		

POTATO AND ONION SOUP

This is a simple but delicious soup that would normally be served as a first course at an Italian meal. However, we love it as a luncheon entree or as the centerpiece for a light supper. The soup tastes best if made with good-quality beef broth.

7 Servings

- 4 cups chopped onions
- 2 garlic cloves, minced
- 2 teaspoons olive oil
- 2 teaspoons butter, *or* non-diet, tub-style canola- or safflower-oil margarine
- 6 cups fat-free, reduced-sodium beef broth, *or* regular defatted beef broth, divided
- 2¼ lbs. boiling potatoes, peeled and cut into ½-in. cubes (6 cups)
- 1½ teaspoons Italian seasoning
- ¼ teaspoon black pepper
- ¼ cup (1 oz.) grated Parmesan cheese
  Salt to taste (optional)

1. In a Dutch oven or similar large, heavy pot, combine onions, garlic, oil, butter, and 3 tablespoons of broth. Cook, uncovered, over medium-high heat, stirring frequently, until onions are softened and begin to brown, about 8 minutes.

2. Add remaining broth, potatoes, Italian seasoning, and pepper. Bring to a boil. Reduce heat, cover, and simmer 10 to 15 minutes or until potatoes are tender.

3. When potatoes are done, use a potato masher to break them up so that the liquid is thickened slightly. Turn off heat under pot. Add cheese a little at a time, stirring to prevent lumps from forming. Salt to taste, if desired, and serve.

Nutritional Data

PER SERVING		EXCHANGES	
Calories:	208	Milk:	0.0
% Calories from fat:	16	Vegetable:	2.0
Fat (gm):	3.7	Fruit:	0.0
Sat. fat (gm):	1.6	Bread:	2.0
Cholesterol (mg):	5.7	Meat:	0.0
Sodium (mg):	375	Fat:	0.5
Protein (gm):	8.9		
Carbohydrate (gm):	35.9		

EASY VENETIAN FISH SOUP

It's surprising how such a simple combination of ingredients can yield such savory results. This makes a good, healthful hurry-up meal.

4 Servings (main dish)

2 teaspoons olive oil
1 teaspoon butter, *or* margarine
1 large garlic clove, minced
1 large onion, chopped
1 large celery stalk, chopped
1 14½-oz. can reduced-sodium chopped tomatoes, including juice, *or* regular chopped tomatoes, including juice
¼ cup dry white wine, *or* sherry
1 8-oz. bottle clam juice
¼ cup chopped parsley leaves plus 2 tablespoons for garnish
1 teaspoon dried marjoram leaves
¼ teaspoon black pepper, *or* to taste
1 lb. fresh or frozen boneless, skinless halibut, red snapper, or other white-fleshed fish, cut into 1-in. chunks
⅛ teaspoon salt, *or* to taste (optional)

1. In a 4-quart pot or saucepan, heat oil and butter to hot, but not smoking, over high heat. Add garlic, onions, and celery. Lower heat slightly, and cook, stirring, until vegetables are well browned, about 6 minutes.

2. Stir in tomatoes, wine, clam juice, ¼ cup parsley, marjoram, and pepper. Reduce heat so mixture simmers gently. Simmer, stirring once or
   twice, for 20 minutes.

3. Add fish; continue simmering a few minutes longer until pieces are
   cooked through and flavors are well blended. Stir in salt, if desired.
   Garnish with remaining 2 tablespoons of parsley.

Nutritional Data

PER SERVING		EXCHANGES	
Calories:	205	Milk:	0.0
% Calories from fat:	27	Vegetable:	2.0
Fat (gm):	6.2	Fruit:	0.0
Sat. fat (gm):	1.3	Bread:	0.0
Cholesterol (mg):	39	Meat:	3.0
Sodium (mg):	172	Fat:	0.0
Protein (gm):	25.9		
Carbohydrate (gm):	9		

CHICKEN-VEGETABLE SOUP WITH ENDIVE

Like spinach and most other greens, curly endive contains a lot of water and loses volume when cooked. As a result, what at first seems to be a large quantity doesn't turn out to be an overabundance at all. The flavor of endive mellows as it cooks, so it adds a pleasing leafy-vegetable taste but no bitterness to the soup.

6 Servings (main dish)

1 tablespoon olive oil
1 large onion, chopped
1 large celery stalk, diced
1 large carrot, diced
2 large garlic cloves, minced
5½ cups fat-free, reduced-sodium chicken broth, *or* defatted regular chicken broth
2 lbs. bone-in chicken breast halves, skin and visible fat removed
1½ teaspoons dried marjoram leaves
½ teaspoon dried basil leaves
½ teaspoon black pepper, *or* to taste
1¼ lbs. (approximately) curly endive (2 medium-sized heads)
2 medium-sized boiling potatoes, peeled and coarsely diced
¼ cup uncooked orzo
1 14½-oz. can reduced-sodium chopped tomatoes, including juice, *or* regular chopped tomatoes, including juice
⅛–¼ teaspoon salt (optional)
2–3 tablespoons freshly grated Parmesan cheese, for garnish

1. In a 4-quart or larger pot or saucepan, heat oil to hot, but not smoking, over high heat. Add onions, celery, carrots, and garlic. Lower heat slightly and cook, uncovered, stirring, until vegetables are lightly browned, about 5 minutes.

2. Stir in broth, chicken breasts, marjoram, basil, and pepper. Reduce heat so mixture simmers gently. Simmer, uncovered, stirring once or twice, for 20 minutes.

3. Meanwhile, pull off and discard tough, outer endive leaves. Coarsely chop the tender, light green endive leaves. Chop enough to yield 5 or 6 cups. Wash, then rewash leaves in a large bowl of water to remove all traces of grit. Transfer to a colander. Rinse several times, then drain thoroughly.

4. Stir potatoes, orzo, and endive into pot. Simmer 5 minutes. Remove chicken breasts from pot. Set aside until cool enough to handle. Stir tomatoes and juice into pot. Simmer until potatoes and orzo are tender and flavors blend, about 10 minutes longer.

5. Meanwhile, pull chicken from bones and cut into bite-sized pieces. Return chicken meat to pot; discard bones. Add salt, if desired. Reheat to piping hot. Serve sprinkled with Parmesan, if desired.

Nutritional Data

PER SERVING		EXCHANGES	
Calories:	284	Milk:	0.0
% Calories from fat:	17	Vegetable:	2.0
Fat (gm):	5.5	Fruit:	0.0
Sat. fat (gm):	1.1	Bread:	1.0
Cholesterol (mg):	61	Meat:	3.0
Sodium (mg):	404	Fat:	0.0
Protein (gm):	31		
Carbohydrate (gm):	27.9		

4
SAUCES AND PASTA

Meat Sauce with Spaghetti

Tomato-Garlic Sauce with Pasta

Marinara Sauce with Pasta

Fresh Tomatoes and Peppers Sauce with Pasta

Mushroom-Tomato Sauce with Pasta

Puttanesca Sauce with Pasta

Eggplant-Mushroom Sauce with Pasta

Creamy Tomatoes and Roasted Peppers Sauce with Pasta

White Clam Sauce with Linguini

Alfredo-Style Sauce with Fettuccini

Ricotta-Spinach Sauce with Pasta

Basil-Chive Pesto and Pasta

MEAT SAUCE WITH SPAGHETTI

When we make spaghetti sauce, we like to prepare enough for several meals. This sauce can be frozen or kept in the refrigerator for up to five days. Notice that we've cut the fat considerably by combining ground round of beef with ground turkey breast. When used in this fashion, the turkey absorbs the flavor of the beef so that the two become indistinguishable. (Be sure to use ground turkey breast, as plain ground turkey usually contains higher-fat dark meat and skin.) In addition, ground vegetables add flavor and texture to the sauce.

8 Servings

Meat Sauce

- 10 ozs. ground round of beef
- 8 ozs. ground turkey breast
- 3 cups chopped onions
- 1 cup coarsely chopped mushrooms
- 2 garlic cloves, minced
- 1 14½-oz. can reduced-sodium tomatoes, including juice, *or* regular tomatoes, including juice
- 2 medium-sized carrots, peeled and grated or shredded
- 2 cups sliced cabbage
- 3 15-oz. cans reduced-sodium tomato sauce, *or* regular tomato sauce
- 3 tablespoons tomato paste
- 2 teaspoons granulated sugar
- 2 teaspoons dried thyme leaves
- 1½ teaspoons dried basil leaves
- ½ teaspoon dried oregano leaves
- 2 bay leaves
- ½ teaspoon salt (optional)
- ¼ teaspoon black pepper

Spaghetti

- 16–18 ozs. uncooked thin spaghetti
  Parmesan cheese, grated, for garnish

1. In a large, heavy pot, combine ground round, ground turkey, onions, mushrooms, and garlic. Cook over medium heat, stirring frequently and breaking up meat with a spoon, until beef is browned.

2. Meanwhile, combine tomatoes and their juice, carrots, and cabbage in a food processor. Process until vegetables have been finely chopped, using on and off bursts to break up any large vegetable pieces. Add vegetable mixture to meat mixture. Add tomato sauce, tomato paste, and sugar, stirring to mix well.

3. Add thyme, basil, oregano, bay leaves, salt, if desired, and pepper. Stir well. Bring to a boil, cover, reduce heat, and simmer 50 to 60 minutes, stirring frequently, until flavors are well blended. Remove bay leaves.

4. Cook spaghetti according to package directions. Arrange individual servings of spaghetti on plates or in wide, shallow bowls. Stir sauce and ladle it over the pasta. Garnish with Parmesan cheese, if desired.

Nutritional Data

PER SERVING		EXCHANGES	
Calories:	437	Milk:	0.0
% Calories from fat:	7	Vegetable:	4.0
Fat (gm):	3.4	Fruit:	0.0
Sat. fat (gm):	0.8	Bread:	3.5
Cholesterol (mg):	28.1	Meat:	1.5
Sodium (mg):	138	Fat:	0.0
Protein (gm):	24.7		
Carbohydrate (gm):	76.4		

TOMATO-GARLIC SAUCE WITH PASTA

This flavorful sauce is easy to double or triple and works well with a variety of pasta shapes. You can keep it in the refrigerator for 3 or 4 days or freeze portions for later use.

4 Servings

Tomato-Garlic Sauce

- 2 tablespoons dry sherry, *or* defatted chicken broth, *or* vegetable broth
- 1 tablespoon olive oil
- 3 garlic cloves, minced
- 1 14½-oz. can reduced-sodium tomatoes, including juice, or regular tomatoes, preferably Italian, including juice, partially pureed in a food processor or finely chopped
- 1 15-oz. can reduced-sodium, *or* regular, tomato sauce
- 2 teaspoons dried oregano leaves
- 2 teaspoons granulated sugar
- ¼ teaspoon salt (optional)
- ⅛ teaspoon black pepper

Pasta

- 8–12 ozs. uncooked penne, *or* other pasta, cooked according to package directions
  Chopped parsley, *or* grated Parmesan cheese, for garnish

1. In a large, heavy saucepan, combine sherry, oil, and garlic. Cook over medium-low heat, stirring frequently, until garlic is golden, 5 to 7 minutes. Add tomatoes, tomato sauce, oregano, sugar, salt, if desired, and pepper. Bring to a boil. Cover, reduce heat, and simmer 20 to 25 minutes.

2. Serve sauce over pasta. Garnish with chopped parsley or grated Parmesan cheese, if desired.

Nutritional Data

PER SERVING		EXCHANGES	
Calories:	334	Milk:	0.0
% Calories from fat:	13	Vegetable:	3.0
Fat (gm):	4.7	Fruit:	0.0
Sat. fat (gm):	0.7	Bread:	3.0
Cholesterol (mg):	0	Meat:	0.0
Sodium (mg):	46	Fat:	1.0
Protein (gm):	10.5		
Carbohydrate (gm):	60.6		

MARINARA SAUCE WITH PASTA

A full-bodied basic sauce, marinara goes together fairly quickly. Not only is it good over plain pasta but it can be served with stuffed shells or over chicken or pork.

4 Servings

Marinara Sauce

1½ tablespoons olive oil, preferably extra-virgin
1 small onion, chopped
2 large garlic cloves, minced
1 28-oz. can reduced-sodium Italian-style tomatoes, including juice, *or* regular Italian-style tomatoes, including juice
3 tablespoons finely chopped fresh basil leaves, *or* 1 tablespoon dried basil leaves
½ teaspoon dried oregano leaves
1 large bay leaf
¼ teaspoon black pepper, *or* to taste
¼ cup tomato paste blended with ¼ cup water
Salt to taste (optional)

Pasta

1 lb. uncooked vermicelli, spaghetti, *or* similar pasta, cooked *al dente* and drained

1. In a very large saucepan or pot over medium-high heat, combine oil and onions. Adjust heat so onions brown but don't burn, and cook, stirring, until lightly browned, about 5 minutes. Add garlic and cook 2

minutes longer. Finely chop tomatoes. Stir tomatoes and their juice, basil, oregano, bay leaf, and pepper into pan.

2. Adjust heat so mixture simmers gently and cook, uncovered, stirring occasionally, about 20 minutes. Stir tomato paste mixture into sauce; cook about 5 minutes longer or until thickened slightly. Discard bay leaf. Spoon sauce over pasta.

Nutritional Data

PER SERVING		EXCHANGES	
Calories:	545	Milk:	0.0
% Calories from fat:	13	Vegetable:	3.0
Fat (gm):	7.8	Fruit:	0.0
Sat. fat (gm):	1.1	Bread:	5.5
Cholesterol (mg):	0	Meat:	0.0
Sodium (mg):	158	Fat:	1.5
Protein (gm):	17.6		
Carbohydrate (gm):	101.9		

FRESH TOMATOES AND PEPPERS SAUCE WITH PASTA

*When produce markets, gardens, and roadside stands are over-
loaded with plump peak-of-season tomatoes and bell peppers,
take advantage of the summer's bounty and prepare this
quick-cooking pasta sauce. It has a wonderful fresh, sprightly
flavor that even the best commercial sauces can't match.*

4 Servings

Tomatoes and Peppers Sauce

    2 tablespoons olive oil, preferably extra-virgin
    2 large garlic cloves, minced
    2 medium-sized onions, finely chopped
 2½ cups coarsely diced red bell peppers
 4¾ cups peeled and very coarsely chopped vine-
         ripened tomatoes (about 2¾ lbs.)
 ¾ teaspoon dried marjoram leaves
 ½ teaspoon dried thyme leaves
 ¼ teaspoon (generous) black pepper
 2½ tablespoons tomato paste
 ¼ teaspoon salt, *or* to taste (optional)

Pasta

   12 ozs. uncooked capellini, vermicelli, *or* similar
         thin pasta, cooked *al dente* and drained

1. In a 12-inch nonstick skillet or saute pan, heat oil to hot, but not
smoking, over high heat. Add garlic, onions, and bell peppers. Cook,
stirring, until vegetables begin to brown, 5 to 7 minutes.

2. Add tomatoes, marjoram, thyme, and black pepper. Boil vigorously for
5 minutes to reduce liquid. Lower heat so mixture simmers; cook,
uncovered, about 20 minutes or until slightly thickened.

3. In a small bowl, stir tomato paste with a little of the pasta sauce until
smoothly incorporated. Return mixture to the skillet. Bring to a simmer. Add salt, if desired. Serve sauce over pasta.

Nutritional Data

PER SERVING		EXCHANGES	
Calories:	524	Milk:	0.0
% Calories from fat:	16	Vegetable:	6.0
Fat (gm):	9.8	Fruit:	0.0
Sat. fat (gm):	1.3	Bread:	4.0
Cholesterol (mg):	0	Meat:	0.0
Sodium (mg):	108	Fat:	2.0
Protein (gm):	16.7		
Carbohydrate (gm):	96.8		

MUSHROOM-TOMATO SAUCE WITH PASTA

The meaty taste of mushrooms comes through clearly in this simple yet substantial sauce. Serve it over pasta for a satisfying vegetarian main dish.

Leftover sauce is also good spooned over steamed green beans, broccoli, or grilled chicken.

4 Servings

Mushroom-Tomato Sauce

    2 tablespoons olive oil, preferably extra-virgin
    5½ cups coarsely sliced mushrooms
    1 large onion, finely chopped
    2 large garlic cloves, minced
    ¼ cup dry red wine
    1 28-oz. can reduced-sodium Italian-style
       chopped tomatoes, including juice, *or* regular
       Italian-style chopped tomatoes, including juice
    ¼ cup tomato paste combined with ½ cup water
    ¾ teaspoon each: dried thyme leaves and dried
       marjoram leaves
    ¼–½ teaspoon black pepper, *or* to taste
    ½ teaspoon salt (optional)

Pasta

    12 ozs. uncooked vermicelli, *or* similar pasta,
        cooked *al dente* and drained

1. In a 12-inch or larger nonstick saute pan or skillet, heat oil to hot, but not smoking, over medium-high heat. Add mushrooms, onions, and garlic; pan will initially be overfull, but mushrooms will gradually lose volume as they cook. Adjust heat so mushrooms and onions cook rapidly but do not burn, and cook, stirring, until juices evaporate and mushrooms are lightly browned, about 7 to 9 minutes.

2. Stir in wine, tomatoes with their juice, tomato paste-water mixture, thyme, marjoram, and pepper.

3. Adjust heat so mixture simmers, and cook, uncovered and stirring occasionally, 20 to 25 minutes until slightly thickened. Add salt, if desired. Spoon over pasta.

Nutritional Data

PER SERVING		EXCHANGES	
Calories:	493	Milk:	0.0
% Calories from fat:	17	Vegetable:	5.0
Fat (gm):	9.4	Fruit:	0.0
Sat. fat (gm):	1.3	Bread:	4.0
Cholesterol (mg):	0	Meat:	0.0
Sodium (mg):	172	Fat:	2.0
Protein (gm):	16.2		
Carbohydrate (gm):	86.4		

PUTTANESCA SAUCE WITH PASTA

*Even if you don't normally bother with reduced-sodium
tomatoes, consider trying them in the following recipe.
Since both the ham and olives have a lot of sodium, the sauce
may be too salty if regular canned tomatoes are used.*

5 Servings

Puttanesca Sauce

- 2 tablespoons olive oil, preferably extra-virgin
- 3 large onions, chopped
- 4 large garlic cloves, minced
- 1 cup finely diced well-trimmed lean ham, *or* Canadian bacon
- 2 28-oz. cans reduced-sodium Italian-style chopped tomatoes, including juice, *or* regular Italian-style chopped tomatoes, including juice
- 1/4 cup finely sliced pitted green olives
- 1 1/2 tablespoons dried oregano leaves
- 1/2 teaspoon black pepper, *or* to taste
- 1/8–1/4 teaspoon hot red pepper flakes, *or* to taste
  Salt to taste (optional)

Pasta

- 1 lb. uncooked vermicelli, spaghetti, *or* similar pasta, cooked *al dente* and drained

1. In a 4-quart or larger pot over medium-high heat, combine oil, onions, and garlic. Adjust heat so onions brown but do not burn, and cook, stirring, until they are golden, 6 or 7 minutes. Stir in ham; cook 2 minutes longer. Stir in tomatoes, olives, oregano, black pepper, and red pepper flakes.

2. Adjust heat so mixture simmers gently and cook, uncovered and stirring occasionally to prevent sticking, about 20 minutes until thickened. Add salt, if desired. Spoon over pasta.

Nutritional Data

PER SERVING		EXCHANGES	
Calories:	551	Milk:	0.0
% Calories from fat:	17	Vegetable:	4.0
Fat (gm):	10.4	Fruit:	0.0
Sat. fat (gm):	1.7	Bread:	4.5
Cholesterol (mg):	8.4	Meat:	1.0
Sodium (mg):	541	Fat:	1.5
Protein (gm):	22.2		
Carbohydrate (gm):	94.1		

EGGPLANT-MUSHROOM SAUCE WITH PASTA

Eggplant and mushrooms go well together in this robust sauce. Both vegetables have a hearty, meaty taste, so this makes a very satisfying vegetarian entree.

4 Servings

Eggplant-Mushroom Sauce

1 medium-sized eggplant, peeled and cut into
³/₄-in. cubes

2 tablespoons olive oil, preferably extra-virgin,
divided

2¹/₂ cups coarsely sliced mushrooms

1 small onion, finely chopped

2 large garlic cloves, minced

2 tablespoons dry white wine, *or* alcohol-free
white wine, *or* water

¹/₃ cup tomato paste combined with 1³/₄ cups vegetable broth, *or* combined with defatted
reduced-sodium chicken broth

³/₄ teaspoon dried marjoram leaves

¹/₄–¹/₂ teaspoon black pepper, *or* to taste

¹/₄–¹/₂ teaspoon salt, *or* to taste (optional)

Pasta

12 ozs. uncooked vermicelli, *or* similar pasta,
cooked *al dente* and drained

1. Spread eggplant cubes in a large microwave-proof pie plate. Sprinkle a tablespoon of water over eggplant. Cover plate with wax paper. Microwave on high power 3 to 4 minutes, stirring after 2 minutes, until pieces are barely tender when tested with a fork. Turn out into a colander and drain well. Pat dry with paper towels.

2. In a 12-inch or larger nonstick saute pan or skillet, heat 1 tablespoon oil to hot, but not smoking, over high heat. Add eggplant and cook, stirring, until lightly browned, about 5 minutes; adjust heat as necessary to prevent burning. Turn out eggplant into a bowl and reserve.

3. Heat remaining 1 tablespoon oil to hot, but not smoking. Add mushrooms, onions, and garlic. Cook, stirring, until mushrooms are lightly browned, about 5 minutes. Stir in wine, tomato paste-broth mixture, marjoram, pepper, and reserved eggplant.

4. Adjust heat so mixture simmers, and cook, uncovered and stirring occasionally, 15 to 20 minutes until mixture is slightly thickened and eggplant is tender when pierced with a fork. Add salt to taste, if desired. Spoon over pasta.

Nutritional Data

PER SERVING		EXCHANGES	
Calories:	476	Milk:	0.0
% Calories from fat:	17	Vegetable:	3.0
Fat (gm):	9	Fruit:	0.0
Sat. fat (gm):	1.2	Bread:	4.5
Cholesterol (mg):	0	Meat:	0.0
Sodium (mg):	216	Fat:	1.5
Protein (gm):	14.4		
Carbohydrate (gm):	84.8		

CREAMY TOMATOES AND ROASTED PEPPERS SAUCE WITH PASTA

Here's a pasta sauce that's quick, easy, and delicious—and so creamy you'd swear it was high in fat. But it's really quite low. The roasted red peppers called for can be purchased in jars at many grocery stores or specialty markets. If unavailable, chopped pimientos can be substituted.

6 Servings

Tomatoes and Roasted Peppers Sauce

- 1/4 cup dry sherry, *or* defatted chicken broth
- 2 teaspoons olive oil
- 1 large onion, chopped
- 2 garlic cloves, minced
- 1 15-oz. can reduced-sodium tomato sauce, *or* regular tomato sauce
- 1 14 1/2-oz. can reduced-sodium tomatoes, including juice, *or* regular tomatoes, including juice
- 1/3 cup coarsely chopped bottled roasted red bell peppers
- 1 tablespoon Italian seasoning
- 2 teaspoons granulated sugar
- 1/4 teaspoon black pepper
- 1/2 cup nonfat sour cream
- 1/2 teaspoon salt, *or* to taste (optional)

Pasta

- 12 ozs. uncooked fusilli (4 cups), cooked according to package directions

1. In a small Dutch oven or similar pot, combine sherry, oil, onions, and garlic. Cook, stirring frequently, until onions are soft, about 5 to 7 minutes.

2. Add tomato sauce and tomatoes, breaking them up with a spoon. Add peppers, Italian seasoning, sugar, and black pepper and stir to mix well. Bring to a boil. Cover, lower heat, and simmer 10 to 15 minutes, stirring occasionally. Turn off heat under pot.

3. Stir in sour cream until well combined. Warm over very low heat an additional 2 minutes. Taste sauce. Add salt, if desired. Serve sauce over pasta. Garnish with parsley, if desired.

Nutritional Data

PER SERVING		EXCHANGES	
Calories:	321	Milk:	0.0
% Calories from fat:	8	Vegetable:	3.0
Fat (gm):	2.7	Fruit:	0.0
Sat. fat (gm):	0.4	Bread:	3.0
Cholesterol (mg):	0	Meat:	0.0
Sodium (mg):	115	Fat:	0.5
Protein (gm):	11.2		
Carbohydrate (gm):	60.4		

WHITE CLAM SAUCE WITH LINGUINI

It's easy to get a quick, tempting meal on the table if you keep some cans of minced clams on hand. This sauce takes only about 15 minutes to cook, during which time the pasta can be readied, too.

4 Servings

White Clam Sauce

  1 tablespoon olive oil, preferably extra-virgin
  1 small onion, finely chopped
  3 large garlic cloves, minced
  2 10¼-oz. cans minced baby clams, juice reserved
  ⅓ cup dry white wine, *or* alcohol-free white wine
  ½ cup finely chopped parsley leaves
  1 teaspoon each: dried oregano, marjoram, and basil leaves
  ¼–½ teaspoon white pepper, *or* to taste
  1 tablespoon butter, *or* non-diet, tub-style margarine
  ¼–½ teaspoon salt (optional)

Pasta

  12 ozs. uncooked linguini, *or* similar pasta, cooked *al dente* and drained

1. In a 12-inch nonstick skillet over high heat, combine oil, onions, and garlic. Lower heat slightly and cook until onions turn translucent and golden, about 5 minutes. Stir in juice drained from clams, wine, parsley, oregano, marjoram, basil, and pepper.

2. Adjust heat so mixture simmers, and cook, uncovered and stirring occasionally, 10 minutes. Add clams, butter, and salt, if desired. Heat until piping hot. Spoon over pasta and serve.

Nutritional Data

PER SERVING		EXCHANGES	
Calories:	477	Milk:	0.0
% Calories from fat:	18	Vegetable:	2.0
Fat (gm):	9.6	Fruit:	0.0
Sat. fat (gm):	2.8	Bread:	4.0
Cholesterol (mg):	98.2	Meat:	2.0
Sodium (mg):	112	Fat:	0.5
Protein (gm):	23.8		
Carbohydrate (gm):	72.9		

ALFREDO-STYLE SAUCE WITH FETTUCCINI

Yes, it's possible to make a delicious reduced-fat version of this famous pasta sauce! Using freshly grated Parmesan will make a significant difference in the taste of the dish.

4 Servings

Alfredo-Style Sauce

- 1 medium-sized onion, finely chopped
- 2 small garlic cloves, minced
- 1/4 cup dry white wine, *or* dry sherry
- 1 tablespoon butter, *or* non-diet canola- or safflower-oil margarine
- 1 1/2 tablespoons cornstarch
- 2 3/4 cups 1% fat milk, divided
- 3/4 cup (3 ozs.) grated Parmesan cheese, preferably freshly grated
- 1/2 cup (2 ozs.) grated nonfat Parmesan cheese topping
- 1/2 cup nonfat sour cream
- 1/4 cup chopped chives, *or* thinly sliced green onion tops
- 1 teaspoon Worcestershire sauce
- 1/2 teaspoon Dijon-style mustard
- 1/8 teaspoon white pepper
  Salt to taste (optional)

Pasta

10–12 ozs. uncooked non-egg fettuccini noodles,
cooked according to package directions

1. In a 12-inch nonstick skillet, combine onions, garlic, wine, and butter. Cook over medium heat, stirring frequently, 6 to 8 minutes or until onions are tender. If liquid begins to evaporate, add a bit of water.

2. In a cup, combine cornstarch with ¼ cup milk, stirring to mix well.

3. Stir remaining 2½ cups of milk into skillet. Bring liquid in pan to a boil. Stir in cornstarch mixture, stirring until mixture thickens. Boil 1 minute, stirring. Reduce heat so that sauce does not boil.

4. Stir in Parmesan cheeses. Stir in sour cream, mixing well and whisking if necessary. Stir in chives, Worcestershire sauce, mustard, and pepper, and stir well. Add salt, if desired. Cook over very low heat an additional 2 or 3 minutes until flavors are well blended.

5. Arrange fettuccini on a serving platter. Top with sauce. Or serve individual portions of sauce over pasta. Garnish with additional chives, if desired.

Nutritional Data

PER SERVING		EXCHANGES	
Calories:	537	Milk:	1.0
% Calories from fat:	20	Vegetable:	0.0
Fat (gm):	11.7	Fruit:	0.0
Sat. fat (gm):	6.7	Bread:	4.5
Cholesterol (mg):	29.4	Meat:	1.0
Sodium (mg):	596	Fat:	1.5
Protein (gm):	29.1		
Carbohydrate (gm):	76.8		

RICOTTA-SPINACH SAUCE WITH PASTA

Simple but surprisingly good and satisfying. For best results,
use a top-quality brand of frozen spinach.

5 Servings

Ricotta-Spinach Sauce

 2 10-oz. packages chopped frozen spinach,
  thawed and drained

 1 tablespoon olive oil, preferably extra-virgin

 2 cups sliced mushrooms

 1 medium-sized onion, finely chopped

 3 large garlic cloves, minced

1 1/4 cups vegetable broth, *or* defatted reduced-
  sodium chicken broth

 1 teaspoon each: dried thyme leaves and dried
  marjoram leaves

 1/4 teaspoon ground nutmeg

1/4–1/2 teaspoon black pepper, *or* to taste

 1 cup nonfat ricotta cheese

 1/3 cup grated Parmesan cheese, preferably
  freshly grated

1/8–1/4 teaspoon salt (optional)

Pasta

 1 lb. uncooked radiatore (wheel-shaped), fusilli,
  or other pasta, cooked barely *al dente* and
  drained

1. A handful at a time, squeeze excess moisture out of spinach. Put
spinach in a medium-sized bowl. Fluff it with a fork, discarding any
tough stem pieces. If spinach is not finely chopped, transfer to a cutting board and chop finely.

2. In a 12-inch or larger nonstick saute pan or skillet, heat oil to hot, but
not smoking, over medium-high heat. Add mushrooms and onions.
Adjust heat so mushrooms and onions cook rapidly but do not burn;
cook, stirring, 3 minutes. Add garlic and continue cooking until mushrooms are lightly browned, 3 or 4 minutes. Stir in broth, spinach,
thyme, marjoram, nutmeg, and pepper.

3. Adjust heat so mixture simmers, and cook, uncovered and stirring occasionally, 5 to 8 minutes or until spinach is tender. Stir in ricotta and Parmesan. Continue cooking just until piping hot; do not boil. Add salt, if desired. Toss sauce with pasta and serve.

Nutritional Data

PER SERVING		EXCHANGES	
Calories:	496	Milk:	0.0
% Calories from fat:	12	Vegetable:	2.0
Fat (gm):	6.8	Fruit:	0.0
Sat. fat (gm):	2	Bread:	5.5
Cholesterol (mg):	5.3	Meat:	1.0
Sodium (mg):	270	Fat:	1.0
Protein (gm):	25.9		
Carbohydrate (gm):	86		

BASIL-CHIVE PESTO AND PASTA

Pesto and pasta make a wonderfully satisfying, rich-tasting combination. The secret to a great pesto is in using fresh, top-quality ingredients such as basil leaves, chives, freshly grated Parmesan, and extra-virgin olive oil. In addition, we've found that toasting nuts increases their flavor significantly, allowing you to use less. So take this easy step before combining ingredients in the food processor.

6 Servings

Pesto

- 3 tablespoons pine nuts (about 1 oz.)
- 3 garlic cloves
- 1½ cups packed fresh basil leaves
- ⅓ cup packed chopped fresh chives, *or* green onions
- 3 tablespoons (½ oz.) freshly grated Parmesan cheese
- 1 tablespoon fresh lemon juice
- ¼ teaspoon (generous) salt, *or* more to taste
- 3 tablespoons extra-virgin olive oil

Pasta

12 ozs. uncooked pasta, such as vermicelli or
    angel hair, cooked according to package
    directions, rinsed, and drained.

1. Spread nuts in a small, nonstick skillet. Cook over medium-high heat,
   stirring constantly, until nuts begin to turn brown and smell toasted,
   about 3 to 4 minutes. Immediately transfer nuts to a plate and cool
   slightly.

2. Combine nuts, garlic, basil, chives, cheese, lemon juice, and salt in a
   food processor. Process until finely minced. With processor on, slowly
   pour olive oil through food tube; process until well blended, stopping
   and scraping down sides of container once or twice. Transfer to a
   small bowl.

3. To serve, toss pesto with pasta. Pesto will keep, tightly sealed, in the
   refrigerator for 2 to 3 days.

Nutritional Data

PER SERVING		EXCHANGES	
Calories:	322	Milk:	0.0
% Calories from fat:	31	Vegetable:	0.0
Fat (gm):	11.4	Fruit:	0.0
Sat. fat (gm):	2	Bread:	3.0
Cholesterol (mg):	2.5	Meat:	0.0
Sodium (mg):	166	Fat:	2.5
Protein (gm):	10.3		
Carbohydrate (gm):	46		

5
MAIN DISHES: MEATS

Beef Braised in Red Wine

Grilled Beef and Vegetable Sandwiches

Home-Style Steak

Meatball Sandwiches

Sicilian Beef and Rice

Spaghetti and Meatballs

Beefy Lasagne

Sausage-and-Peppers Lasagne

Pork with Peppers and Zucchini

Quick Pepperoni-Vegetable-Pasta Skillet

BEEF BRAISED IN RED WINE

The original Italian recipe for this delicious oven dinner was made with a roast. But we've substituted round steak because it's leaner and cooks faster. A good quality Chianti works well in the recipe. However, you can substitute any table-quality dry red wine. Be sure to use flavorful beef broth, as it adds to the richness of the dish.

6 Servings

- 1 lb. beef round steak, trimmed of all fat and cut into bite-sized strips
- 2 tablespoons all-purpose white flour
- 1 large onion, chopped
- 2 garlic cloves, minced
- 2 cups sliced mushrooms
- 1 cup fat-free, reduced-sodium beef broth, *or* regular defatted beef broth, divided
- 2 teaspoons olive oil
- 2 large celery stalks, thinly sliced
- 2 large carrots, peeled and thinly sliced
- 1 15-oz. can reduced-sodium tomato sauce, *or* regular tomato sauce
- 1 cup dry red wine
- 1 teaspoon dried thyme leaves
- 2 large bay leaves
- 1/2 teaspoon dry mustard
- 1/4 teaspoon salt, *or* to taste (optional)
- 1/8 teaspoon black pepper
- 1/8 teaspoon ground celery seed
- 5 medium-sized baking potatoes, peeled and cut into large chunks

1. Preheat oven to 350 degrees. In a large, shallow baking pan, combine beef and flour, stirring until meat is coated. Bake 12 to 15 minutes, stirring occasionally so that meat browns on all sides and any leftover flour coats meat. Remove and set aside.

2. Meanwhile, in a flame-proof, oven-proof Dutch oven or similar large pot, combine onions, garlic, mushrooms, 1/4 cup broth, and oil. Cook

over medium heat, stirring frequently, until vegetables are tender, about 10 minutes.

3. Add celery and carrots along with tomato sauce, wine, remaining broth, and reserved beef. Add thyme, bay leaves, mustard, salt, if desired, pepper, and celery seed. Stir to mix well. Add potatoes, stirring them into sauce. Bring to a simmer.

4. Cover, transfer pot to oven, and bake 1 hour or until beef is tender. Remove and discard bay leaves. Serve in large bowls.

Nutritional Data

PER SERVING		EXCHANGES	
Calories:	316	Milk:	0.0
% Calories from fat:	12	Vegetable:	3.0
Fat (gm):	4.4	Fruit:	0.0
Sat. fat (gm):	1.1	Bread:	2.0
Cholesterol (mg):	36.5	Meat:	2.0
Sodium (mg):	116	Fat:	0.0
Protein (gm):	20		
Carbohydrate (gm):	43.3		

GRILLED BEEF AND VEGETABLE SANDWICHES

For a festive luncheon or supper entree, let diners make their own marinated flank steak sandwiches. To enrich the flavor, we cook the onions from the marinade with other vegetables and use them to garnish the sandwich.

4 Servings (main dish)

Marinade and Meat

- $1/3$ cup fresh lemon juice
- $1/3$ cup fat-free, reduced-sodium chicken broth, *or* regular defatted chicken broth
- 1 tablespoon olive oil
- 1 large onion, coarsely chopped
- 2 large garlic cloves, minced
- 1 tablespoon Italian seasoning
- $1/4$ teaspoon salt (optional)
- 3–4 drops hot pepper sauce
- 1 lb. flank steak, trimmed of all fat

Vegetables

- 3 bell peppers, preferably red, yellow, and green, seeded and sliced
- 3 ripe tomatoes, sliced
- $1/4$ teaspoon salt (optional)
- $1/4$ teaspoon black pepper

To serve

- 1 loaf Italian bread, sliced and lightly toasted

1. *For marinade and meat:* In a shallow glass baking dish, combine lemon juice, broth, oil, onions, garlic, Italian seasoning, salt, if desired, and hot pepper sauce. Stir to mix well. Place meat in baking dish. Spoon some marinade and onions over top. Cover and refrigerate 12 hours or up to 24 hours, turning and basting with marinade and onions once or twice.

2. Adjust rack 5 inches from broiler. Preheat broiler. Transfer meat to a nonstick broiler pan coated with cooking spray. Broil meat 11 to 16 minutes, turning once, until desired degree of doneness is reached.

3. *Vegetables:* Meanwhile, with a slotted spoon, remove onions from marinade and transfer to a nonstick skillet. Add peppers and 3 tablespoons of marinade. Discard remaining marinade. Cook over medium high to high heat, 4 or 5 minutes or until onions and peppers begin to char. Sprinkle tomatoes with salt, if desired, and black pepper.

4. *To serve:* Slice meat on the diagonal and arrange on a serving platter. Arrange onions-peppers mixture and tomatoes on separate serving plates. Place bread in a basket. Let diners make their own sandwiches.

Nutritional Data

PER SERVING		EXCHANGES	
Calories:	566	Milk:	0.0
% Calories from fat:	22	Vegetable:	2.0
Fat (gm):	14	Fruit:	0.0
Sat. fat (gm):	4.7	Bread:	4.0
Cholesterol (mg):	50.7	Meat:	3.0
Sodium (mg):	739	Fat:	1.5
Protein (gm):	41.6		
Carbohydrate (gm):	67.4		

HOME-STYLE STEAK

◆

Here's round steak in an easy tomato sauce. To complete the meal,
add a green vegetable such as broccoli florets or sliced zucchini.

4 Servings

12 ozs. round steak, trimmed of all fat and cut
   into thin strips
1/4 teaspoon salt (optional)
1/8 teaspoon black pepper
1 large onion, chopped
2 garlic cloves, minced
1/4 cup fat-free, reduced-sodium beef broth, *or*
   regular defatted beef broth
2 teaspoons olive oil
1 14 1/2-oz. can reduced-sodium tomatoes,
   including juice, *or* regular canned tomatoes,
   including juice
1 8-oz. can reduced-sodium tomato sauce, *or*
   regular tomato sauce
1 teaspoon dried basil leaves
1/4 teaspoon dried thyme leaves
8 ozs. uncooked thin spaghetti or other pasta,
   cooked according to package directions

1. Sprinkle round steak with salt, if desired, and pepper. In a 12-inch
   nonstick skillet coated with cooking spray, cook round steak over
   medium heat until browned on all sides, 4 to 5 minutes. Remove with a
   slotted spoon, and reserve in a medium bowl.

2. In same skillet, combine onions, garlic, broth, and oil. Cook over medium heat, stirring frequently, until onions are tender, 5 to 6 minutes.

3. Return meat to pan. Add tomatoes, breaking them up with a spoon.
   Add tomato sauce, basil, and thyme. Stir to mix well. Bring to a boil.
   Reduce heat, cover, and simmer 35 to 40 minutes until meat is tender.
   Remove cover and simmer an additional 5 minutes to cook down
   sauce slightly.

4. To serve, arrange pasta on individual serving plates. Top with meat
   and sauce.

Nutritional Data

PER SERVING		EXCHANGES	
Calories:	396	Milk:	0.0
% Calories from fat:	15	Vegetable:	3.0
Fat (gm):	6.4	Fruit:	0.0
Sat. fat (gm):	1.5	Bread:	3.0
Cholesterol (mg):	41	Meat:	2.0
Sodium (mg):	94	Fat:	0.0
Protein (gm):	26.1		
Carbohydrate (gm):	57.6		

MEATBALL SANDWICHES

For many families, meatball sandwiches are a favorite lunch or light dinner entree. With our meatball recipe on page 70, you can enjoy them often.

6 Servings (main dish)

1 recipe Meatballs (page 70)
1 26-oz. jar reduced-fat, reduced-sodium marinara sauce, *or* our reduced-fat marinara sauce (page 45)
1 cup sliced onions
2 cups sliced mushrooms
1 small green bell pepper, seeded and chopped
1 small garlic clove, minced
1/4 teaspoon Italian seasoning
6 Kaiser rolls, *or* 6-in. submarine sandwich buns
1 cup (4 ozs.) shredded reduced-fat mozzarella cheese

1. Make recipe for meatballs on page 70 according to directions, except make 24 slightly larger balls (1 rounded tablespoon each) and bake 15 to 18 minutes, stirring once or twice. Combine meatballs with marinara sauce. Cover and simmer 10 to 15 minutes.

2. Meanwhile, place onions, mushrooms, peppers, garlic, Italian seasoning, and 1 tablespoon water in a microwave-proof medium bowl. Stir to mix. Cover with wax paper, and microwave on high power 5 to 6 minutes or until vegetables are tender; stir once during microwaving. Remove wax paper and allow steam to escape. Drain liquid from vegetables.

3. Cut rolls in halves, and place 2 halves on each plate. Divide the meat-
    ball-sauce mixture evenly among the rolls, covering only one half-roll
    on each plate. Sprinkle 2½ tablespoons of mozzarella over sauce and
    meatballs on each sandwich. Top with vegetable mixture, dividing
    evenly. Close sandwiches. Serve with knives and forks.

Nutritional Data

PER SERVING		EXCHANGES	
Calories:	452	Milk:	0.0
% Calories from fat:	18	Vegetable:	4.0
Fat (gm):	8.9	Fruit:	0.0
Sat. fat (gm):	1.8	Bread:	3.0
Cholesterol (mg):	56.6	Meat:	2.0
Sodium (mg):	664	Fat:	0.5
Protein (gm):	27.3		
Carbohydrate (gm):	63.9		

SICILIAN BEEF AND RICE

Instead of serving meat sauce with pasta, try this tasty variation using rice. Note that we've combined ground beef round and ground turkey breast to lower the fat in the dish. Mixed in this way, the turkey takes on the taste of the beef, so no one will even know it's there.

4 Servings

- 1 large onion, chopped
- 2 garlic cloves, minced
- 1 large green bell pepper, seeded and diced
- 6 ozs. ground round of beef
- 5 ozs. ground turkey breast
- 2 15-oz. cans reduced-sodium tomato sauce, *or* regular tomato sauce
- 1 cup chopped cabbage
- 1 teaspoon each: dried basil leaves and dried thyme leaves
- 1 large bay leaf
- $1/4$ teaspoon salt (optional)
- $1/8$ teaspoon black pepper
- 1 cup uncooked long-grain white rice, cooked according to package directions
- $1/4$ cup (1 oz.) grated Parmesan cheese

1. In a 12-inch nonstick skillet, combine onions, garlic, green peppers, ground round of beef, and ground turkey breast. Cook over medium heat until beef has browned and onions are tender, 5 or 6 minutes. Stir in tomato sauce, cabbage, basil, thyme, bay leaf, salt, if desired, and pepper. Bring to a boil. Reduce heat, and simmer 25 to 30 minutes, stirring occasionally. Remove and discard bay leaf.

2. To serve, place rice in a deep serving bowl. Ladle over one-third of sauce. Sprinkle with grated cheese. Toss gently with two forks until rice is mixed with sauce and cheese. Top individual portions with remaining sauce.

Nutritional Data

PER SERVING		EXCHANGES	
Calories:	391	Milk:	0.0
% Calories from fat:	11	Vegetable:	4.0
Fat (gm):	4.5	Fruit:	0.0
Sat. fat (gm):	2	Bread:	2.5
Cholesterol (mg):	39.2	Meat:	2.0
Sodium (mg):	215	Fat:	0.0
Protein (gm):	24.6		
Carbohydrate (gm):	61.1		

SPAGHETTI AND MEATBALLS

If you like your pasta dinners with meatballs, add these to your favorite sauce. They're especially good with a double recipe of Tomato-Garlic Sauce (page 44). We've cut the fat dramatically by combining ground round of beef with ground turkey breast. Mixed in this manner, the turkey takes on a beefy flavor and is virtually undetectable. Note that the recipe calls specifically for ground turkey breast, as it is far leaner than ordinary ground turkey. To eliminate fat for browning the meatballs, we pop them in the oven while we attend to other tasks. The recipe calls for commercial pasta sauce so your meal can be on the table in a hurry.

6 Servings

Meatballs

- 9 ozs. ground round of beef
- 6 ozs. ground turkey breast
- 1/4 cup fine breadcrumbs made from slightly stale white or wholewheat bread
- 1 small onion, finely chopped
- 1 garlic clove, minced
- 2 teaspoons Italian seasoning
- 1 large egg white
- 1/2 teaspoon salt (optional)
- 1/8 teaspoon black pepper

Sauce and Pasta

- 6 cups (2, 26-oz. jars) fat-free, reduced-sodium pasta sauce, *or* regular reduced-fat pasta sauce
- 16 ozs. uncooked thin spaghetti

1. *For meatballs:* Preheat oven to 400 degrees. Coat a shallow baking pan with cooking spray. Set aside.

2. In a large bowl, combine ground round, ground turkey, breadcrumbs, onions, garlic, Italian seasoning, egg white, salt, if using, and pepper. Mix well. Roll into 30, 1-inch balls. Place balls in prepared pan. Bake 10 to 15 minutes, stirring once, until meatballs are browned on all sides. If meatballs seem greasy, turn out onto a plate lined with paper towels to blot excess fat.

3. *For sauce and pasta:* Heat sauce in a Dutch oven or similar large, heavy pot. When meatballs are browned, transfer to sauce, and simmer 20 minutes.

   Cook pasta according to package directions. Serve individual servings of meatballs and sauce over pasta.

Nutritional Data

PER SERVING		EXCHANGES	
Calories:	550	Milk:	0.0
% Calories from fat:	9	Vegetable:	4.5
Fat (gm):	5.6	Fruit:	0.0
Sat. fat (gm):	0.9	Bread:	4.5
Cholesterol (mg):	56.6	Meat:	2.0
Sodium (mg):	224	Fat:	0.0
Protein (gm):	29.8		
Carbohydrate (gm):	91.7		

BEEFY LASAGNE

Fresh parsley lends pleasing flavor and texture to this hearty lasagne, which is much leaner than standard versions. One way we've reduced the fat is by combining ground turkey breast and ground round of beef. We've found that when the two are blended in this manner, the turkey takes on the flavor of the beef.

6 Servings

12 ozs. uncooked lasagne noodles
 8 ozs. ground round of beef
 5 ozs. ground turkey breast
 1 large onion, chopped
 1 garlic clove, minced
1½ cups sliced fresh mushrooms
 3 15-oz. cans reduced-sodium tomato sauce, *or* regular tomato sauce
 1 tablespoon plus 1 teaspoon Italian seasoning
    Pinch of black pepper
1½ cups nonfat ricotta cheese
 4 ozs. (1 cup loosely packed) shredded reduced-fat mozzarella cheese, divided
 4 ozs. (1 cup loosely packed) shredded nonfat mozzarella cheese, divided
1½ cups chopped parsley leaves
 3 tablespoons (³⁄₄ oz.) grated Parmesan cheese

1. Preheat oven to 375 degrees. Cook noodles barely *al dente,* according to package directions. Rinse and drain in a colander.

2. Meanwhile, in a Dutch oven or similar large pot, cook ground round, ground turkey, onions, garlic, and mushrooms over medium heat until beef is brown and onions are soft, 5 to 6 minutes. With a large spoon, skim and discard any fat. Add tomato sauce, Italian seasoning, and pepper. Bring to a boil. Reduce heat and simmer about 5 minutes.

3. Place a thin layer of sauce on the bottom of a 9½-in. x 13-in. baking pan, spreading it evenly with the back of a large spoon. Arrange a layer of lasagne noodles over sauce, overlapping slightly. Top noodles with ricotta cheese, spreading it out evenly with the back of a large spoon.

4. In a small bowl, mix together mozzarella cheeses. Sprinkle one third of mozzarella cheese mixture evenly on top of ricotta. Add another layer of sauce, another layer of noodles, another third of the mozzarella, and

the parsley. Add a thin layer of sauce. Top with the last noodles and then remaining sauce. Reserve remaining third of mozzarella and Parmesan.

5. Bake in preheated oven 35 to 40 minutes, until lasagne is heated through and beginning to bubble. Sprinkle with remaining mozzarella and Parmesan cheeses, and bake an additional 2 minutes until cheese is partially melted. Let stand for 5 minutes before cutting into 6 or 8 portions.

Note: Lasagne can be made one or two days ahead, covered, and refrigerated until reheated and served.

Nutritional Data

PER SERVING		EXCHANGES	
Calories:	419	Milk:	0.0
% Calories from fat:	15	Vegetable:	4.0
Fat (gm):	7.2	Fruit:	0.0
Sat. fat (gm):	1.9	Bread:	2.0
Cholesterol (mg):	29.9	Meat:	3.0
Sodium (mg):	457	Fat:	0.0
Protein (gm):	38		
Carbohydrate (gm):	52.6		

SAUSAGE-AND-PEPPERS LASAGNE

This full-flavored lasagne features a handy shortcut—ready-to-use bottled roasted red bell peppers. To trim preparation time even further, you can use a good-quality, low-fat commercial pasta sauce in place of our homemade Tomato-Garlic Sauce (page 44).

9 Servings

- 1 12-oz. package reduced-fat turkey-and-pork bulk sausage
- 2 large onions, chopped
- 1 1/2 cups sliced fresh mushrooms (optional)
- 2 large garlic cloves, minced
- 3 cups Tomato-Garlic Sauce (page 44), *or* reduced-fat commercial meatless pasta sauce
- 1 12-oz. jar roasted red bell peppers, drained and chopped
- 2 15-oz. cartons nonfat ricotta cheese
- 1 8-oz. package shredded reduced-fat mozzarella cheese, divided
- 1/4 cup grated Parmesan cheese
- 8 ozs. uncooked lasagne noodles, cooked *al dente* and well-drained

1. Preheat oven to 350 degrees. Lightly coat a 3-quart lasagne pan, or flat rectangular glass or similar oven-proof casserole, with cooking spray.

2. In a 12-inch nonstick skillet over medium-high heat, stir together sausage, onions, mushrooms, if using, and garlic. Cook, breaking up meat with a spoon, 7 to 10 minutes or until onions and sausage are lightly browned.

3. Turn out sausage mixture onto a double thickness of paper towels. Blot away all excess fat. Return mixture to skillet. Stir in pasta sauce and roasted peppers. Return to burner and heat until piping hot; set aside.

4. In a large bowl, stir together ricotta, half of mozzarella, and Parmesan; reserve remaining mozzarella for garnish.

5. Spread a thin layer of tomato-meat sauce in casserole. Top with a layer of noodles, followed by half of ricotta mixture, then with a thin layer of sauce. Add another layer of noodles, remainder of ricotta, and thin layer of sauce. Top with remaining noodles, then all remaining sauce.

6. Bake on center oven rack 35 to 45 minutes until lasagne is bubbly and cooked through. Sprinkle reserved mozzarella cheese over top. Return to oven. Heat 5 minutes longer or until cheese is melted and bubbly.

Nutritional Data

PER SERVING		EXCHANGES	
Calories:	425	Milk:	0.0
% Calories from fat:	21	Vegetable:	4.0
Fat (gm):	10	Fruit:	0.0
Sat. fat (gm):	4	Bread:	2.0
Cholesterol (mg):	35.6	Meat:	3.0
Sodium (mg):	729	Fat:	0.0
Protein (gm):	33.7		
Carbohydrate (gm):	52.3		

PORK WITH PEPPERS AND ZUCCHINI

In Italy this recipe would be made with whole pork chops.
To reduce the fat, we've cut boneless pork loin into strips.

4 Servings

1 lb. pork tenderloin, trimmed of all fat and cut into strips
1/4 teaspoon salt (optional)
1/8 teaspoon black pepper
3 tablespoons dry sherry, *or* defatted chicken broth
2 teaspoons olive oil
1 large onion, chopped
1 garlic clove, minced
1 15-oz. can reduced-sodium tomato sauce, *or* regular tomato sauce
2 cups frozen mixed green, red, and yellow bell peppers
1 1/2 cups thinly sliced zucchini
3/4 teaspoon each: dried basil and dried thyme leaves
1 bay leaf
Additional salt and pepper, to taste
8 ozs. (2 1/2 cups) uncooked cut fusilli, cooked according to package directions

1. Sprinkle pork with salt, if desired, and pepper. In a nonstick skillet coated with cooking spray, cook pork strips over medium heat, turning frequently, until they begin to brown. With a slotted spoon remove to a medium-sized bowl and set aside.

2. Add sherry, oil, onions, and garlic to pan. Scrape up any browned bits from pan bottom. Cook over medium heat, stirring frequently, 5 or 6 minutes or until onions are tender. If liquid begins to evaporate, add more sherry.

3. Return pork to pan. Add tomato sauce, frozen peppers, zucchini, basil, thyme, and bay leaf.

4. Raise heat and bring liquid to a boil. Lower heat and simmer, covered, 15 minutes. Remove bay leaf. Taste sauce and add additional salt and

pepper, if desired. Serve individual portions of pork and vegetables over pasta.

Nutritional Data

PER SERVING		EXCHANGES	
Calories:	480	Milk:	0.0
% Calories from fat:	15	Vegetable:	4.0
Fat (gm):	7.8	Fruit:	0.0
Sat. fat (gm):	1.9	Bread:	3.0
Cholesterol (mg):	65.4	Meat:	3.0
Sodium (mg):	91	Fat:	0.0
Protein (gm):	34.8		
Carbohydrate (gm):	63.9		

QUICK PEPPERONI-VEGETABLE-PASTA SKILLET

Pepperoni is a fatty ingredient, but, fortunately, it is also so flavorful that a little goes a long way. For convenience, buy a 3-ounce, presliced package.

4 Servings

1 1/2 teaspoons olive oil, preferably extra-virgin
1 large onion, coarsely chopped
1/2 cup coarsely chopped red bell pepper
2 large garlic cloves, minced
3 ozs. sliced pepperoni, coarsely diced (about 2/3 cup)
1/3 cup fat-free, reduced-sodium chicken broth, *or* defatted regular chicken broth
1 14 1/2-oz. can reduced-sodium Italian-style chopped tomatoes, including juice, *or* regular Italian-style chopped tomatoes, including juice
3/4 teaspoon each: dried oregano leaves and dried marjoram leaves
1/4–1/2 teaspoon black pepper, *or* to taste
3 cups small broccoli florets
1 1/3 cups (7 ozs.) uncooked small macaroni, cooked barely *al dente* and drained
1 1/2 tablespoons grated Parmesan cheese

1. In a 12-inch or larger nonstick saute pan or skillet, heat oil to hot, but not smoking, over high heat. Add onions and peppers. Lower heat slightly and cook, stirring, until vegetables are lightly browned, about 5 minutes. Stir in garlic and pepperoni; cook 2 minutes longer.

2. Add broth, tomatoes, oregano, marjoram, and pepper and simmer, uncovered, 10 minutes. Stir in broccoli; cook until almost tender, 3 to 5 minutes longer. Stir in macaroni and Parmesan. Simmer several minutes longer until broccoli is cooked through and flavors have blended.

Nutritional Data

PER SERVING		EXCHANGES	
Calories:	390	Milk:	0.0
% Calories from fat:	30	Vegetable:	3.0
Fat (gm):	13.3	Fruit:	0.0
Sat. fat (gm):	4.3	Bread:	2.5
Cholesterol (mg):	1.9	Meat:	1.0
Sodium (mg):	538	Fat:	2.0
Protein (gm):	16.2		
Carbohydrate (gm):	53.5		

6
MAIN DISHES: POULTRY

Chicken Cacciatore

Chicken Breasts with Rosemary

Chicken Risotto

Chicken-Pasta Skillet with Sun-Dried Tomatoes and Olives

Braised Chicken with Red Wine

Braised Turkey Stew, Milan Style

Country Turkey Ragout with White Wine

Turkey Marsala with Mushrooms

Turkey Cutlets with Sage

Turkey with Lemon-Caper Sauce

CHICKEN CACCIATORE

Classic chicken cacciatore recipes sometimes call for 4 or 5 table-spoons—or even more—of fat. As this updated version proves, it's possible to keep all the flavor and still cut fat by 60 to 80 percent.

5 Servings

1¹/₃ lbs. boneless, skinless chicken breast meat, trimmed of fat and cut into 1-in. cubes

¹/₄ teaspoon salt, divided

¹/₄ cup all-purpose white flour

1¹/₂ tablespoons olive oil

2 large garlic cloves, minced

2 medium-sized onions, chopped

1 medium-sized carrot, coarsely diced

2 cups mixed ³/₄-in. red and green bell pepper chunks

1 14¹/₂-oz. can reduced-sodium Italian-style chopped tomatoes, including juice, *or* regular Italian-style chopped tomatoes, including juice

1¹/₂–2 cups fat-free, reduced-sodium chicken broth, *or* defatted regular chicken broth

³/₄ teaspoon each: dried thyme leaves and dried marjoram leaves

¹/₄–¹/₂ teaspoon black pepper, *or* to taste

¹/₄ cup tomato paste combined with ¹/₄ cup water

1. Set oven rack about 4 inches from broiler, and preheat broiler to highest heat. Coat a medium-sized rimmed baking sheet with nonstick cooking spray.

2. Sprinkle chicken with ¹/₈ teaspoon salt. Combine chicken and flour in a paper or plastic bag. Close and shake until cubes are coated. Spread chicken evenly on baking sheet. Broil chicken cubes 5 to 9 minutes until lightly browned, watching carefully and stirring frequently to prevent burning. Remove pan from oven and reserve.

3. Heat oil to hot, but not smoking, over high heat in a nonstick 12-inch skillet or saute pan. Add garlic, onions, carrots, and peppers. Cook over high heat, stirring, until vegetables begin to brown, 5 to 7 minutes.

4. Add tomatoes, broth, thyme, marjoram, and pepper. Boil for 3 or 4 minutes to reduce liquid slightly. Lower heat so mixture simmers gently. Add chicken cubes to skillet. Cover and cook, stirring occasionally

to prevent sticking, until chicken is tender and flavors are well blended, about 25 minutes. If necessary to prevent sticking, thin mixture with a little more broth.

5. Stir in tomato paste mixture. Simmer several minutes longer. Add remaining 1/8 teaspoon salt.

Nutritional Data

PER SERVING		EXCHANGES	
Calories:	291	Milk:	0.0
% Calories from fat:	24	Vegetable:	3.0
Fat (gm):	7.9	Fruit:	0.0
Sat. fat (gm):	1.5	Bread:	0.5
Cholesterol (mg):	73.6	Meat:	3.5
Sodium (mg):	393	Fat:	0.0
Protein (gm):	32.1		
Carbohydrate (gm):	23.8		

CHICKEN BREASTS WITH ROSEMARY

Easy yet elegant, this zesty, healthful entree can be on the table in about 30 minutes. It's good served along with a risotto and simple vegetable dish or salad.

4 Servings

1½ teaspoons olive oil
1 teaspoon balsamic vinegar
2 large garlic cloves, minced
Zest (yellow part of peel) of 1 medium-sized lemon, finely grated
⅛ teaspoon black pepper
4 4-oz. boneless, skinless chicken breast halves
⅓ cup dry white wine, *or* alcohol-free white wine, *or* defatted reduced-sodium chicken broth
¼ teaspoon finely chopped fresh rosemary, *or* ½ teaspoon finely crumbled dried rosemary
½ cup peeled and diced fresh tomato
¼ teaspoon salt (optional)

1. In a medium-sized bowl, stir together oil, vinegar, garlic, lemon zest, and pepper. Add chicken, tossing to coat, and let stand for 10 minutes.

2. Lightly coat a nonstick 12-inch skillet or saute pan with cooking spray. Heat skillet over medium-high heat until drops of water sizzle when sprinkled on the surface. Immediately add chicken pieces and seasoning mixture. Adjust heat so chicken sears and cooks rapidly but does not burn. Cook, turning frequently, until well-browned on all sides.

3. Add wine and rosemary to skillet. Lower heat so mixture simmers gently. Cook 10 minutes; if necessary add 2 or 3 tablespoons water to prevent skillet from boiling dry. Add tomatoes and continue gently simmering until chicken is just cooked through, 6 to 8 minutes longer. If skillet is nearly dry, stir in several tablespoons of water to produce a little sauce. Add salt, if desired. Serve with sauce and bits of tomato spooned over chicken breast halves.

Nutritional Data

PER SERVING		EXCHANGES	
Calories:	173	Milk:	0.0
% Calories from fat:	25	Vegetable:	0.0
Fat (gm):	4.7	Fruit:	0.0
Sat. fat (gm):	1.1	Bread:	0.0
Cholesterol (mg):	69	Meat:	3.0
Sodium (mg):	64	Fat:	0.0
Protein (gm):	25.6		
Carbohydrate (gm):	2.4		

CHICKEN RISOTTO

Risotto is made with arborio rice, which cooks to a wonderfully creamy texture. Prepared conventionally, risotto must be stirred frequently and watched carefully. But our microwave method eliminates all that work.

5 Servings

Risotto

> 1 cup uncooked arborio rice
>
> 3¹⁄₃ cups fat-free, reduced-sodium chicken broth, *or* defatted regular chicken broth, divided
>
> ¹⁄₄ teaspoon white pepper

Chicken and Vegetables

> 12 ozs. boneless, skinless chicken breast halves, trimmed of all fat and cut into small bite-sized pieces
>
> ¹⁄₄ teaspoon salt (optional)
>
> ¹⁄₈ teaspoon black pepper
>
> 1¹⁄₄ teaspoons dried thyme leaves, divided
>
> 2 teaspoons olive oil
>
> ¹⁄₄ cup fat-free, reduced-sodium chicken broth, *or* regular defatted chicken broth
>
> ¹⁄₄ cup dry white wine, *or* sherry
>
> ¹⁄₄ teaspoon saffron threads
>
> ¹⁄₂ teaspoon dried oregano leaves
>
> 1¹⁄₂ cups frozen mixed green, red, and yellow bell peppers
>
> 1 cup frozen green peas

1. *For risotto:* In a 3-quart microwave-proof casserole, combine rice and 3 tablespoons broth. Microwave, uncovered, 60 seconds on high power. Stir well. Add remaining broth and white pepper. Stir to mix well. Cover with casserole lid and microwave, 8 to 9 minutes. Stir well. Uncover and microwave an additional 12 to 14 minutes or until most of liquid is absorbed and rice is tender. Allow to stand 2 to 3 minutes.

2. *For chicken and vegetables:* Meanwhile, sprinkle chicken with salt, if desired, black pepper, and 1/2 teaspoon thyme. In a 12-inch nonstick skillet, combine chicken and oil. Cook over medium heat, turning chicken pieces frequently until they begin to brown, 4 to 5 minutes.

3. To skillet, add broth, wine, saffron, remaining thyme, and oregano. Stir in frozen peppers and peas. Bring to a boil, reduce heat, cover, and simmer 12 to 15 minutes. Stir chicken mixture into risotto and serve.

Nutritional Data

PER SERVING		EXCHANGES	
Calories:	316	Milk:	0.0
% Calories from fat:	13	Vegetable:	1.0
Fat (gm):	4.4	Fruit:	0.0
Sat. fat (gm):	0.8	Bread:	2.5
Cholesterol (mg):	41.4	Meat:	2.0
Sodium (mg):	306	Fat:	0.0
Protein (gm):	23.6		
Carbohydrate (gm):	41.7		

CHICKEN-PASTA SKILLET WITH SUN-DRIED TOMATOES AND OLIVES

◆

Sun-dried tomatoes and oil-cured black olives lend a rich, earthy flavor to this colorful one-dish meal. If you happen to have left-over cooked rigatoni, ziti, or other sturdy tube-shaped pasta on hand, you can use 2 1/2 cups of it to replace the uncooked pasta called for in this recipe.

5 Servings

- 2 teaspoons olive oil, preferably extra-virgin
- 1/2 cup each: chopped onions and green bell peppers
- 1 lb. boneless, skinless chicken breast halves, cut into 1-in. pieces
- 1 medium-sized zucchini, coarsely cubed
- 1 cup chopped canned tomatoes, including juice
- 1 teaspoon dried marjoram leaves
- 1/3 cup fat-free, reduced-sodium chicken broth, *or* defatted regular chicken broth
- 3 tablespoons diced oil-packed sun-dried tomatoes
- 1 tablespoon finely chopped, pitted oil-cured black olives, *or* Greek black olives
- 1/4 teaspoon salt (optional)
- 1 1/2 cups (about 4 ozs.) uncooked rigatoni, *or* other medium-sized tube-shaped pasta, cooked barely *al dente* and drained

1. In a 12-inch nonstick skillet, combine oil, onions, and peppers over medium-high heat. Cook, stirring, about 4 minutes or until onions soften. Stir in chicken and cook, stirring, about 3 minutes longer or until chicken pieces are almost cooked through.

2. Stir in zucchini, tomatoes, and marjoram; cook 1 minute longer. Stir in broth, sun-dried tomatoes, olives, and salt, if desired, until well mixed. Add pasta and cook until heated through, about 5 minutes longer.

Nutritional Data

PER SERVING		EXCHANGES	
Calories:	252	Milk:	0.0
% Calories from fat:	21	Vegetable:	1.0
Fat (gm):	5.9	Fruit:	0.0
Sat. fat (gm):	1.1	Bread:	1.5
Cholesterol (mg):	55.2	Meat:	2.0
Sodium (mg):	217	Fat:	0.0
Protein (gm):	24.8		
Carbohydrate (gm):	24.5		

BRAISED CHICKEN WITH RED WINE

Traditionally, this recipe was used to prepare rabbit, but it also works well with ordinary chicken breasts. It is vaguely reminiscent of the well-known French chicken-and-red wine classic, coq au vin.

4 Servings

- 2 teaspoons extra-virgin olive oil
- 1 medium-sized onion, chopped
- 2 large garlic cloves, minced
- 4 4-oz. boneless, skinless chicken breast halves
- 3/4 cup fat-free, reduced-sodium chicken broth, *or* regular defatted chicken broth
- 3/4 cup Chianti, *or* other dry Italian red wine
- 1 large bay leaf
- 1 1/2 teaspoons dried oregano leaves
- 1/2 teaspoon dried thyme leaves
- 1/4 teaspoon (scant) black pepper
- 1/4 teaspoon salt (optional)

1. In a 12-inch nonstick skillet or stir-fry pan, combine oil, onions, and garlic over medium-high heat. Cook, stirring, until onions are limp and begin to brown, about 5 minutes. Add chicken breast halves and cook 6 to 8 minutes longer, turning to brown lightly all over; add a tablespoon of broth if necessary to prevent burning.

2. Add remaining broth, wine, bay leaf, oregano, thyme, pepper, and salt, if desired, to pan. Simmer, uncovered, 15 to 18 minutes or until

chicken pieces are just cooked through. Remove chicken and set aside. Raise heat to highest setting; boil mixture until reduced to about ¼ cup.

3. Return reserved chicken to pan. Heat until piping hot. Remove bay leaf. Serve with liquid spooned over each piece.

Nutritional Data

PER SERVING		EXCHANGES	
Calories:	207	Milk:	0.0
% Calories from fat:	24	Vegetable:	1.0
Fat (gm):	5.3	Fruit:	0.0
Sat. fat (gm):	1.2	Bread:	0.0
Cholesterol (mg):	69	Meat:	3.0
Sodium (mg):	152	Fat:	0.0
Protein (gm):	26.8		
Carbohydrate (gm):	4.7		

BRAISED TURKEY STEW, MILAN STYLE

This recipe recalls the tangy flavor of osso buco, the Italian classic dish featuring veal shanks braised in wine. However, we've substituted turkey breast cubes for the veal and simplified the preparation. Instead of cooking the sauce on top of the stove and stirring frequently, simply bake the stew in the oven for 50 minutes, and serve over rice.

5 Servings

1¼ lbs. skinless turkey breast meat, cut into bite-sized pieces
2 teaspoons olive oil
3 tablespoons all-purpose white flour
1 large onion, chopped
2 garlic cloves, minced
1¼ cups dry white wine, divided
1 cup fat-free, reduced-sodium beef broth, *or* regular defatted beef broth
1 8-oz. can reduced-sodium tomato sauce, *or* regular tomato sauce
8 baby carrots, cut in half, *or* 2 medium carrots, peeled and sliced
2 celery stalks, thinly sliced
¼ cup chopped parsley leaves
1½ teaspoons dried thyme leaves
2 large bay leaves
3 strips lemon zest (yellow part of peel), each ½ in. x 3 in.
¼ teaspoon (generous) salt, *or* to taste (optional)
¼ teaspoon black pepper
1½ cups uncooked long-grain white rice, cooked according to package directions.

1. Preheat oven to 375 degrees. In a large, shallow baking pan, combine turkey and oil. Stir to coat. Add flour. Stir to coat turkey with flour. Bake 13 to 15 minutes, stirring occasionally so that turkey begins to brown and any leftover flour coats pieces. Remove and set aside. Lower oven heat to 350 degrees.

2. Meanwhile, in a large flame-proof, oven-proof Dutch oven or similar large pot, combine onions, garlic, and ¹/₄ cup of wine. Cook over medium heat, stirring frequently, until onions are tender, 5 or 6 minutes. Add broth, remaining wine, tomato sauce, reserved turkey, carrots, celery, parsley, thyme, bay leaves, lemon zest, salt, if desired, and black pepper. Stir to mix well. Bring to a simmer. Cover, transfer pot to oven, and bake 50 minutes or until turkey is tender.

3. Remove lemon zest and bay leaves. Serve individual portions of stew over rice.

Nutritional Data

PER SERVING		EXCHANGES	
Calories:	434	Milk:	0.0
% Calories from fat:	10	Vegetable:	2.0
Fat (gm):	4.9	Fruit:	0.0
Sat. fat (gm):	1.2	Bread:	3.0
Cholesterol (mg):	44	Meat:	3.0
Sodium (mg):	99	Fat:	0.0
Protein (gm):	26.7		
Carbohydrate (gm):	59.5		

COUNTRY TURKEY RAGOUT WITH WHITE WINE

The original version of this dish featured veal, but we've lowered the fat by using turkey breast cubes instead. Interestingly, the switch is so successful that most people don't even notice the change.

5 Servings

1½ lbs. boneless, skinless turkey breast, cut into 1-in. cubes

⅓ cup all-purpose white flour

2 tablespoons plus ½ teaspoon olive oil

2 large garlic cloves, minced

1 large onion, chopped

2 large carrots, coarsely diced

1 large celery stalk, cut into ¼-in. slices

2½ cups coarsely sliced mushrooms

1 15-oz. can reduced-sodium Italian-style tomatoes, including juice, *or* regular Italian-style tomatoes, including juice

½ cup dry white wine

About ¼ cup fat-free, reduced-sodium chicken broth, *or* regular defatted chicken broth

Pinch each: crumbled dried rosemary and sage

¼ teaspoon black pepper, *or* to taste

⅛ teaspoon salt (optional)

1. Combine turkey and flour in a paper or plastic bag. Close and shake until cubes are coated.

2. Heat 1 tablespoon oil to hot, but not smoking, over medium-high heat in a nonstick 12-inch skillet. Add half of turkey cubes; cook, stirring frequently, until nicely browned, about 5 minutes. Set aside. Add 1 more tablespoon oil and remaining turkey to pan. Repeat browning process. Set turkey aside.

3. Add remaining half-teaspoon of oil to skillet. Add garlic, onions, carrots, celery, and mushrooms. Cook over high heat, stirring, until vegetables begin to brown, about 6 minutes.

4. Return turkey to skillet, along with tomatoes, wine, broth, rosemary, sage, and pepper. Reduce heat so mixture simmers very gently. Tightly cover skillet (with foil if necessary) and cook, stirring occasionally,

until turkey is tender and flavors are well blended, 35 to 40 minutes. If necessary, thin mixture with a little more chicken broth. Add salt to taste, if desired, and serve.

Nutritional Data

PER SERVING		EXCHANGES	
Calories:	278	Milk:	0.0
% Calories from fat:	30	Vegetable:	2.0
Fat (gm):	9.3	Fruit:	0.0
Sat. fat (gm):	1.8	Bread:	0.5
Cholesterol (mg):	52.8	Meat:	3.0
Sodium (mg):	95	Fat:	0.0
Protein (gm):	26.7		
Carbohydrate (gm):	18.3		

TURKEY MARSALA WITH MUSHROOMS

In this recipe turkey cutlets stand in for veal with great results. A nonstick skillet makes it possible to saute the turkey cutlets and mushrooms with a fraction of the fat used in the traditional veal version.

The recipe calls for smashing the garlic cloves before chopping so their juice can infuse the turkey more readily.

4 Servings

- 1 lb. skinless turkey breast cutlets
- 2 teaspoons lemon juice
- 2 large garlic cloves, peeled, smashed, and chopped
- 4 tablespoons all-purpose flour
- 2 teaspoons olive oil, divided
- 2 teaspoons butter, divided
- 1/4 teaspoon salt, divided
- 1/4 cup finely chopped onions
- 2 cups coarsely sliced mushrooms
- 1/2 cup dry marsala wine
- 1/2 cup fat-free, reduced-sodium chicken broth, *or* regular defatted chicken broth
  Pinch of black pepper, *or* to taste
- 1 tablespoon finely chopped fresh parsley leaves (optional)
  Lemon wedges, for garnish

1. Lay cutlets on sheet of plastic wrap. Sprinkle with lemon juice. Sprinkle garlic over cutlets. Cover cutlets with plastic wrap. Using a kitchen mallet or back of a large, heavy spoon, pound each cutlet until 1/8 inch thick. Let stand a few minutes. Lay cutlets on wax paper. Dust with half of flour. Turn over and dust with remaining flour. Preheat oven to 200 degrees.

2. In a 12-inch nonstick skillet, heat 1/2 teaspoon oil and 1/2 teaspoon butter over medium-high heat until hot, but not smoking. Add half of the cutlets, along with half of the salt. Cook on one side until lightly browned, about 1 1/2 minutes. Turn over and cook on other side until lightly browned and just cooked through, about 2 minutes longer.

Transfer cutlets to an oven-proof serving dish. Cover and let stand in oven. Add ½ teaspoon more oil and ½ teaspoon more butter to skillet. Heat until hot. Add remaining cutlets and salt. Repeat cooking process with second batch. Transfer cutlets to oven.

3. Add remaining oil and butter, then onions and mushrooms to skillet. Adjust heat so mixture cooks rapidly and cook, stirring, about 4 to 6 minutes or until mushrooms are browned and most juice has evaporated from pan. Stir wine, broth, and pepper into pan. Cook over high heat, stirring, until liquid is reduced by half.

4. Remove cutlets from oven, and pour mushroom mixture over them. Garnish with parsley, if desired. Serve immediately, along with lemon wedges, if desired.

Nutritional Data

PER SERVING		EXCHANGES	
Calories:	209	Milk:	0.0
% Calories from fat:	30	Vegetable:	2.0
Fat (gm):	6.8	Fruit:	0.0
Sat. fat (gm):	2.1	Bread:	0.0
Cholesterol (mg):	49.1	Meat:	3.0
Sodium (mg):	255	Fat:	0.0
Protein (gm):	21.9		
Carbohydrate (gm):	9.8		

TURKEY CUTLETS WITH SAGE

Sage is often paired with poultry in Italian cooking.
It adds a robust flavor and aroma to this dish.

4 Servings

4 teaspoons red wine vinegar
2 large garlic cloves, smashed and chopped
2 teaspoons finely crumbled dried sage leaves
1 lb. skinless turkey breast cutlets
4 tablespoons all-purpose flour
2 teaspoons olive oil, divided
1½ teaspoons butter, *or* non-diet, tub-style margarine, divided
¼ teaspoon salt, divided
½ cup fat-free, reduced-sodium chicken broth, *or* regular defatted chicken broth
1 tablespoon fresh lemon juice
Pinch of black pepper, *or* to taste

1. Lay out a large sheet of plastic wrap. Sprinkle half of vinegar, half of garlic, and half of sage on plastic wrap. Place cutlets on plastic wrap. Sprinkle remaining vinegar, garlic, and sage over cutlets. Cover cutlets with second sheet of plastic wrap. Using a kitchen mallet or back of a large, heavy spoon, pound cutlets to flatten and embed garlic and sage. Let stand 5 minutes.

2. Lay cutlets on clean sheet of plastic wrap or wax paper. Dust with half of the flour. Turn over and dust with remaining flour. Preheat oven to 200 degrees.

3. In a 12-inch nonstick skillet, heat 1 teaspoon oil and 1 teaspoon butter over medium-high heat until hot, but not smoking. Add half of the cutlets, along with half of the salt. Cook on one side until lightly browned, about 1½ minutes. Turn over and cook on second side until browned and just cooked through, about 2 to 3 minutes longer. Transfer cutlets to an oven-proof serving dish. Cover, and let stand in oven.

4. Add 1 teaspoon remaining oil and ½ teaspoon remaining butter to skillet. Heat until hot. Add remaining cutlets and salt. Repeat cooking process with second batch. Transfer cutlets to oven.

5. Stir broth, lemon juice, and pepper into pan. Cook over high heat, stirring, until liquid is reduced by half. Pour mixture over cutlets. Serve immediately.

Nutritional Data

PER SERVING		EXCHANGES	
Calories:	173	Milk:	0.0
% Calories from fat:	33	Vegetable:	0.0
Fat (gm):	6.2	Fruit:	0.0
Sat. fat (gm):	2	Bread:	0.0
Cholesterol (mg):	47.8	Meat:	3.0
Sodium (mg):	229	Fat:	0.0
Protein (gm):	20.9		
Carbohydrate (gm):	7.4		

TURKEY WITH LEMON-CAPER SAUCE

In Italy, this dish would be made with veal cutlets. We've substituted turkey to reduce the fat. The delicate combination of lemon and capers works well with turkey.

4 Servings

1 lb. skinless turkey cutlets
2 tablespoons white flour
1/4 teaspoon dried thyme leaves
1/4 teaspoon salt (optional)
1/4 teaspoon white pepper
2 teaspoons olive oil, divided
1 garlic clove, minced, divided
1 cup fat-free, reduced-sodium chicken broth, *or* regular defatted chicken broth
2 teaspoons lemon juice
1 tablespoon capers

1. Preheat oven to 200 degrees. Lay cutlets on wax paper. Dust with half of flour. Turn and dust with remaining flour. Sprinkle thyme, salt, if desired, and pepper evenly over cutlets.

2. In a 12-inch nonstick skillet, combine one-half of oil and garlic. Add half of cutlets. Over medium-high heat, cook on one side until lightly browned, about 1 1/2 minutes. Turn and cook on second side until lightly browned and just cooked through, about 2 minutes longer. Remove cutlets to a shallow oven-proof casserole. Cover and let stand in oven. Add remaining oil and remaining garlic to skillet. Add remaining cutlets and repeat cooking process. Transfer cutlets to oven.

3. Stir broth and lemon juice into pan. Stir in capers. Cook over high heat, stirring, until liquid is reduced by half. Remove cutlets from oven, and pour sauce over them. Garnish with parsley, if desired. Or serve turkey and sauce on a bed of pasta.

Nutritional Data

PER SERVING		EXCHANGES	
Calories:	147	Milk:	0.0
% Calories from fat:	30	Vegetable:	0.0
Fat (gm):	4.7	Fruit:	0.0
Sat. fat (gm):	1.1	Bread:	0.0
Cholesterol (mg):	44	Meat:	3.0
Sodium (mg):	202	Fat:	0.0
Protein (gm):	21		
Carbohydrate (gm):	3.9		

7
MAIN DISHES: SEAFOOD

Tuna Steaks with Sweet-and-Sour Tomato Relish

Salmon Risotto

Mediterranean-Style Sole

Braised Fish with Sun-Dried Tomato Sauce

Florentine Fish Dinner

Baked Stuffed Fish with Wine

Fish Stew with Marsala Wine

Shrimp with Artichokes and Peppers

Scallops, Shrimp, and Peppers Over Pasta

Shrimp and Rice

TUNA STEAKS WITH SWEET-AND-SOUR TOMATO RELISH

*Spicy tomato relish nicely complements grilled tuna
in this easy but elegant recipe.*

4 Servings

Tuna

> 1 teaspoon olive oil
> 1 small garlic clove, minced
> 1/2 teaspoon lemon juice
> 1/4 teaspoon each: dried thyme and basil leaves
> 1/8 teaspoon salt (optional)
> 1/8 teaspoon black pepper
> 1 lb. tuna steak, thickly sliced

Relish

> 2 tablespoons tomato paste
> 1 1/2 tablespoons red wine vinegar
> 1 teaspoon water
> 1 1/2 tablespoons granulated sugar
> 1 teaspoon olive oil
> 1/4 teaspoon each: dried thyme and basil leaves
> 1 large tomato, seeded and cubed

1. *For tuna:* Preheat broiler. In a cup, stir together oil, garlic, lemon juice, thyme, basil, salt, if desired, and black pepper. Coat broiler pan with cooking spray. Place fish on pan. Drizzle oil and lemon mixture over fish and spread it evenly.

2. Broil fish about 5 inches from heat for 8 minutes. Turn with a broad spatula, and broil an additional 7 to 10 minutes or until flesh has turned white and is cooked through.

3. *For relish:* Meanwhile, in a medium-sized bowl, combine tomato paste, vinegar, and water. Stir to mix well. Add sugar, oil, thyme, and basil. Set aside.

4. Just before fish is cooked through, in a small nonstick skillet coated with cooking spray, sear tomatoes briefly over high heat. Stir into sauce.

5. *To serve:* Serve tuna on individual plates or serving platter. Pass tomato relish.

Nutritional Data

PER SERVING		EXCHANGES	
Calories:	174	Milk:	0.0
% Calories from fat:	18	Vegetable:	1.0
Fat (gm):	3.5	Fruit:	0.0
Sat. fat (gm):	0.6	Bread:	0.0
Cholesterol (mg):	49.4	Meat:	3.0
Sodium (mg):	108	Fat:	0.0
Protein (gm):	26.5		
Carbohydrate (gm):	8.5		

SALMON RISOTTO

This rich and flavorful dish makes a wonderful centerpiece for a company meal. Prepared the conventional way, it would be a time-consuming task. But with our method, you can prepare the salmon and sauce while the risotto cooks in the microwave oven.

6 Servings

Risotto

    1 cup uncooked arborio rice
    2 teaspoons olive oil
 3¹/₃ cups fat-free, reduced-sodium chicken broth,
      or defatted regular chicken broth

Salmon

  12 ozs. boneless Atlantic salmon fillet, cut into 4-in. pieces
 ¹/₂ cup sliced green onions
 ¹/₄ cup chopped parsley leaves
 ¹/₄ cup dry sherry
  2 teaspoons olive oil
 ³/₄ cup 1% fat milk
 ²/₃ cup nonfat sour cream
  2 teaspoons dried dill, *or* 1 tablespoon fresh dill
  1 teaspoon dry mustard
 ¹/₂ teaspoon salt (optional)
 ¹/₄ teaspoon white pepper

1. *For risotto:* In a 3-quart microwave-proof casserole, combine rice and oil. Microwave, uncovered, 60 seconds on high power. Stir well. Add broth and stir to mix well. Cover with casserole lid and microwave 8 to

9 minutes. Stir well. Microwave an additional 8 minutes. Stir. Uncover and microwave an additional 4 to 5 minutes or until most of liquid is absorbed and rice is tender. Allow to stand 2 to 3 minutes or until ready to combine with salmon in Step 5.

2. *For salmon:* While risotto cooks, in a large nonstick skillet coated with cooking spray, cook salmon over medium heat, breaking up large pieces, until cooked through, 9 to 11 minutes. Remove from pan, remove skin, flake, and set aside.

3. In pan in which salmon was cooked, combine onions, parsley, sherry, and oil. Cook over medium heat, stirring frequently, 3 to 4 minutes until onions and parsley are just cooked. Remove from heat.

4. In a 2-cup measure, combine milk and sour cream and whisk until smooth. Add dill, mustard, salt, if desired, and pepper and stir to mix. Stir into onion mixture until well combined. Stir in reserved salmon. Cook over low heat, 3 minutes, stirring frequently.

5. Stir salmon mixture into risotto. Garnish with dill sprigs or chopped fresh parsley, if desired.

Nutritional Data

PER SERVING		EXCHANGES	
Calories:	282	Milk:	0.0
% Calories from fat:	23	Vegetable:	0.0
Fat (gm):	7.2	Fruit:	0.0
Sat. fat (gm):	1.2	Bread:	2.0
Cholesterol (mg):	31.6	Meat:	2.0
Sodium (mg):	246	Fat:	0.0
Protein (gm):	18.8		
Carbohydrate (gm):	32.1		

MEDITERRANEAN-STYLE SOLE

Try this for a fast and flavorful skillet dinner. The recipe features sole, but you can substitute any lean mild-flavored white fish such as flounder, halibut, or turbot. Directions call for cooking the vegetables and then the fish in the same skillet. Or to reduce preparation time, ready the fish in a separate skillet while the vegetables are cooking.

4 Servings

- ½ cup dry-packed sun-dried tomatoes
- 7–9 ozs. uncooked penne rigate, *or* other similar pasta shape
- 1 16-oz. bag frozen red, green, and yellow bell peppers and onions
- ½ cup fat-free, reduced-sodium chicken broth, *or* regular defatted chicken broth
- 2 teaspoons olive oil
- 2 garlic cloves, minced
- 1 teaspoon dried basil leaves
- ⅓ cup grated nonfat Parmesan cheese topping
- ¼ teaspoon salt (optional)
- ⅛ teaspoon black pepper
- 1 lb. skinless fillets of sole

1. In a 1-cup measure or small bowl, cover tomatoes with hot water and let stand 5 to 10 minutes. Drain and chop.

2. Cook pasta according to package directions. Rinse and drain in a colander.

3. Meanwhile, in a 12-inch nonstick skillet, combine peppers-onions mixture, broth, reserved tomatoes, oil, garlic, and basil. Stir to mix well. Cook, uncovered, over medium to medium-high heat 10 to 12 minutes, stirring frequently, until onions are very tender. Stir in Parmesan. Stir pasta into vegetable mixture. Transfer to a serving platter and keep warm.

4. Rinse out and dry skillet in which vegetables were cooked. Coat with cooking spray. Sprinkle salt, if desired, and black pepper evenly over fish. In batches if necessary, add fish to pan, and cook over medium

heat until cooked through, 3 to 6 minutes, depending on thickness. Top pasta-vegetable mixture with fillets and serve.

Nutritional Data

PER SERVING		EXCHANGES	
Calories:	387	Milk:	0.0
% Calories from fat:	11	Vegetable:	2.0
Fat (gm):	4.9	Fruit:	0.0
Sat. fat (gm):	0.8	Bread:	3.0
Cholesterol (mg):	59.8	Meat:	3.0
Sodium (mg):	306	Fat:	0.0
Protein (gm):	33.2		
Carbohydrate (gm):	52.9		

BRAISED FISH WITH SUN-DRIED TOMATO SAUCE

The combination of tomato sauce and sun-dried tomatoes gives this dish rich color and flavor. It's very quick and easy to prepare.

4 servings

- 1 tablespoon olive oil
- 2 large garlic cloves, minced
- 1 large onion, chopped
- 1 cup fat-free, reduced-sodium chicken broth, *or* regular defatted chicken broth
- 3 tablespoons chopped oil-packed sun-dried tomatoes
- 1 teaspoon dried marjoram leaves
- 1/2 teaspoon dried oregano leaves
- 1/4 teaspoon black pepper, *or* to taste
- 1 1/4 lbs. fresh or frozen boneless, skinless halibut, red snapper, or similar firm white-fleshed fish, cut into 4 serving pieces
- 1 8-oz. can reduced-sodium tomato sauce, *or* regular tomato sauce
- 1/4 teaspoon salt (optional)

1. Heat oil to hot, but not smoking, over medium heat in a 12-inch non-stick skillet. Add garlic and onions. Cook, stirring, until onions are well-browned, about 6 minutes.

2. Stir in chicken broth, sun-dried tomatoes, marjoram, oregano, and pepper. Adjust heat and boil vigorously, uncovered stirring once or twice, until liquid is reduced to about 2 tablespoons, about 4 minutes.

3. Add fish and tomato sauce. Simmer a few minutes longer, just until pieces are cooked through and flavors are well blended. Stir in salt, if desired.

Nutritional Data

PER SERVING		EXCHANGES	
Calories:	243	Milk:	0.0
% Calories from fat:	28	Vegetable:	2.0
Fat (gm):	7.4	Fruit:	0.0
Sat. fat (gm):	1	Bread:	0.0
Cholesterol (mg):	45.5	Meat:	3.5
Sodium (mg):	192	Fat:	0.0
Protein (gm):	32.5		
Carbohydrate (gm):	10.3		

FLORENTINE FISH DINNER

*We like to make this quick and easy recipe with flounder,
but you can substitute any lean, mild-favored white fish
such as sole, halibut, or turbot.*

4 Servings

2½ cups uncooked fusilli, *or* similar pasta shape

¼ teaspoon salt (optional)

⅛ teaspoon black pepper

1 lb. skinless, mild, white fish fillets such as
flounder, turbot, or cod

1 14-oz. can reduced-sodium stewed tomatoes,
or regular stewed tomatoes

1 10-oz. package frozen chopped spinach,
thawed

2 teaspoons olive oil

2 teaspoons Italian seasoning

1 garlic clove, minced

½ teaspoon salt, *or* to taste (optional)

⅛ teaspoon black pepper

2 tablespoons (½ oz.) grated Parmesan cheese,
divided

1. Preheat oven to 200 degrees. Cook pasta according to package directions. Rinse and drain in a colander.

2. Coat a nonstick skillet with cooking spray. Sprinkle salt, if desired, and black pepper evenly over fish. In batches if necessary, add fish to pan, and cook over medium heat until cooked through, 2 to 4 minutes per side, depending on thickness. Remove fish to an oven-proof dish. Cover and set aside in oven to keep warm.

3. Rinse out and dry skillet in which fish was cooked. In skillet, combine tomatoes, spinach, oil, Italian seasoning, garlic, salt, if desired, and pepper. Stir to mix well. Bring to a boil. Lower heat, and cook uncovered 4 to 5 minutes or until sauce has cooked down slightly and spinach is tender.

4. Arrange pasta on a serving platter. Top with one-half of Parmesan. Top with tomato-spinach mixture and then with the reserved fish. Sprinkle remaining Parmesan over all.

Nutritional Data

PER SERVING		EXCHANGES	
Calories:	416	Milk:	0.0
% Calories from fat:	13	Vegetable:	1.5
Fat (gm):	5.9	Fruit:	0.0
Sat. fat (gm):	1.4	Bread:	3.0
Cholesterol (mg):	62.3	Meat:	3.0
Sodium (mg):	211	Fat:	0.0
Protein (gm):	33.5		
Carbohydrate (gm):	56.4		

BAKED STUFFED FISH WITH WINE

Here's a quick and easy fish dinner. We start the vegetables in the microwave to reduce their preparation time and also eliminate the fat that would be needed if they were cooked on the stove top. Check nutritional information on stuffing-mix packages, as some have considerably more fat than others.

4 Servings

- 1 large onion, chopped
- 1 garlic clove, minced
- 2½ cups (6 ozs.) fresh mushrooms, sliced
- 2 tablespoons fat-free, reduced-sodium chicken broth, *or* regular defatted chicken broth
- 1½ cups crumb-type *seasoned* stuffing mix
- ¼ cup (1 oz.) grated nonfat Parmesan cheese topping
- 1 lb. skinless, lean, white fish fillets such as turbot, flounder, or cod
- ¼ teaspoon dried basil leaves
- ¼ teaspoon salt (optional)
- ¼ teaspoon black pepper
- ¼ cup dry white wine

1. Preheat oven to 375 degrees. In a 2½-quart microwave-proof, oven-proof casserole, stir together onions, garlic, mushrooms, and chicken broth. Cover with casserole lid or wax paper. Microwave on high power 5 to 6 minutes or until onions are tender; stop and stir once during microwaving. Remove from microwave oven, and stir in stuffing mix and Parmesan.

2. Sprinkle fish with basil, salt, if desired, and pepper. Arrange fish on top of stuffing mixture, cutting fillets to fit and overlapping if necessary. Pour wine over fish. Cover and bake 20 to 25 minutes or until fish flakes easily with a fork.

Nutritional Data

PER SERVING		EXCHANGES	
Calories:	188	Milk:	0.0
% Calories from fat:	7	Vegetable:	1.0
Fat (gm):	1.4	Fruit:	0.0
Sat. fat (gm):	0.2	Bread:	0.5
Cholesterol (mg):	48.6	Meat:	3.0
Sodium (mg):	278	Fat:	0.0
Protein (gm):	25.3		
Carbohydrate (gm):	16.2		

FISH STEW WITH MARSALA WINE

While marsala wine is often used in Italian recipes, it is not often paired with fish. It adds a distinctive, appealing note to this simple fish stew.

4 Servings

 1 tablespoon olive oil, preferably extra-virgin
 1 large onion, chopped
 1 cup coarsely chopped mixed red and green bell peppers
 $1/2$ cup coarsely chopped celery
 2 large garlic cloves, minced
 $2^{1/4}$ cups fat-free, reduced-sodium chicken broth, *or* regular defatted chicken broth
 $1/3$ cup dry marsala wine
 $3/4$ teaspoon dried thyme leaves
 1 large bay leaf
 $1/8$ teaspoon cayenne pepper, *or* to taste
 2 cups ($5^{1/2}$ ozs.) uncooked medium-sized pasta shells, cooked barely *al dente* and drained
 $1/4$ cup tomato paste blended with $1/4$ cup water
 2 tablespoons fresh lemon juice
 $1/4$ teaspoon salt (optional)
 1 lb. boneless, skinless haddock, *or* other mild white fish, fillets, cut into chunks

1. In a 12-inch, deep-sided nonstick skillet or 13-inch saute pan, over high heat, combine oil, onions, bell peppers, and celery. Reduce heat slightly, and cook, stirring, 3 minutes. Add garlic and cook until onions are browned, about 3 minutes longer. Add broth, marsala, thyme, bay leaf, and cayenne.

2. Bring to a boil and cook, uncovered, 10 minutes. Stir in pasta, along with tomato paste mixture, lemon juice, and salt, if desired.

3. Add fish; simmer 3 to 4 minutes until fillets are opaque and flake when touched with a fork. Serve in soup plates or bowls.

Nutritional Data

PER SERVING		EXCHANGES	
Calories:	359	Milk:	0.0
% Calories from fat:	13	Vegetable:	2.0
Fat (gm):	5.3	Fruit:	0.0
Sat. fat (gm):	0.8	Bread:	2.0
Cholesterol (mg):	64.6	Meat:	3.0
Sodium (mg):	424	Fat:	0.0
Protein (gm):	31.2		
Carbohydrate (gm):	43.7		

SHRIMP WITH ARTICHOKES AND PEPPERS

This skillet dish is quick, easy, and brimming with flavor.

4 Servings

1   13 ³/₄-oz. can artichoke hearts, drained
2   teaspoons olive oil
1   large onion, chopped
1   large garlic clove, minced
3   tablespoons dry white wine, *or* sherry, *or* defatted, reduced-sodium chicken broth
³/₄   teaspoon dried thyme leaves
1   15-oz. can reduced-sodium tomato sauce, *or* regular tomato sauce
1¹/₂   cups frozen mixed green, red, and yellow bell peppers
¹/₈   teaspoon salt, *or* to taste (optional)
¹/₈   teaspoon black pepper
12   ozs. peeled medium-sized fresh shrimp
8   ozs. uncooked penne, *or* other similar pasta shapes, cooked according to package directions

1. Cut artichoke hearts into quarters if necessary. Remove and discard any tough outer leaves. Set aside.

2. In a 12-inch skillet, combine oil, onions, garlic, wine, and thyme. Cook over medium heat, stirring frequently, until onions are tender, about 5 or 6 minutes. If liquid begins to evaporate, add a bit of water. Add tomato sauce, reserved artichokes, frozen peppers, salt, if desired, and black pepper. Stir to mix well. Bring to a boil, reduce heat, cover, and simmer 5 minutes.

3. Add shrimp and simmer an additional 4 or 5 minutes until pink and curled. Serve individual portions of shrimp and vegetable mixture over pasta. Garnish with parsley, if desired.

Nutritional Data

PER SERVING		EXCHANGES	
Calories:	526	Milk:	0.0
% Calories from fat:	9	Vegetable:	4.0
Fat (gm):	5.7	Fruit:	0.0
Sat. fat (gm):	1	Bread:	5.0
Cholesterol (mg):	131.2	Meat:	2.0
Sodium (mg):	338	Fat:	0.0
Protein (gm):	33.7		
Carbohydrate (gm):	88.7		

SCALLOPS, SHRIMP, AND PEPPERS OVER PASTA

A light, colorful medley that goes together quickly.
If desired, you can use all scallops or all shrimp instead
of a combination in this dish.

4 Servings

2 tablespoons olive oil

2 cups mixed (red, green, yellow, etc.) 1-in. bell pepper chunks

1 large onion, coarsely chopped

2 large garlic cloves, minced

1½ cups bottled clam juice, *or* defatted low-sodium chicken broth

⅓ cup chopped fresh parsley leaves

1½ tablespoons fresh lemon juice

1 teaspoon grated lemon zest (yellow part of peel)

½ teaspoon dried thyme leaves

Pinch of dried hot red pepper flakes

1 large ripe tomato, peeled, cored, and coarsely chopped

8 ozs. peeled medium-sized fresh shrimp

8 ozs. bay scallops, *or* sea scallops, cut into bite-sized pieces

¼ teaspoon salt, *or* to taste (optional)

12 ozs. uncooked vermicelli, *or* other thin pasta, cooked *al dente* and drained

1. In a 12-inch nonstick skillet, heat oil to hot, but not smoking, over high heat. Add peppers, onions, and garlic. Lower heat slightly, and cook, stirring, until peppers and onions begin to brown, about 6 minutes. Turn out into a bowl and reserve.

2. To skillet previously used, add broth, parsley, lemon juice, zest, thyme, and pepper flakes. Adjust heat so mixture boils rapidly and cook, uncovered, stirring once or twice, until liquid is reduced to about 3 tablespoons. Add tomatoes; boil 3 or 4 minutes longer or until soft.

3. Add shrimp, scallops, and reserved vegetables. Cook about 3 minutes longer or just until shrimp are curled and scallops barely cooked through. Remove from heat. Add salt, if desired. Serve over the pasta.

Nutritional Data

PER SERVING		EXCHANGES	
Calories:	544	Milk:	0.0
% Calories from fat:	16	Vegetable:	5.0
Fat (gm):	9.9	Fruit:	0.0
Sat. fat (gm):	1.3	Bread:	4.0
Cholesterol (mg):	111.6	Meat:	2.0
Sodium (mg):	342	Fat:	0.5
Protein (gm):	33.9		
Carbohydrate (gm):	80.3		

SHRIMP AND RICE

◆

Here's an easy, flavorful, dinner entree prepared the Sicilian way, with the rice cooked separately and then combined with the shrimp and sauce. To avoid using extra dishes, the recipe calls for a flame-proof casserole for the rice. However, you could substitute a large saucepan, and then stir the cooked rice into the skillet with the shrimp before transferring the mixture to a serving dish.

5 Servings

$1^{1}/_{2}$ cups uncooked white rice

1 medium-sized onion, chopped

1 celery stalk, diced

1 15-oz. can reduced-sodium tomato sauce, *or* regular tomato sauce

$^{1}/_{2}$ cup chopped parsley leaves

1 tablespoon olive oil

2 garlic cloves, minced

1 teaspoon each: dried thyme, basil, and oregano leaves

$^{1}/_{4}$ teaspoon salt (optional)

$^{1}/_{4}$ teaspoon black pepper

$1^{1}/_{4}$ lbs. peeled medium-sized fresh shrimp, *or* frozen and thawed shrimp

1. In a flame-proof $2^{1}/_{2}$-quart casserole, combine rice, onions, and celery. Stir in 3 cups of water. Cover, and bring to a boil. Reduce heat, and simmer 15 to 20 minutes until rice is tender.

2. After rice has cooked 10 minutes, in a 12-inch skillet, combine tomato sauce, parsley, oil, garlic, thyme, basil, oregano, salt, if desired, and pepper. Stir to mix well.

3. Stir in shrimp. Bring to a boil. Cover, reduce heat, and simmer, stirring occasionally, 4 to 6 minutes or until shrimp have turned pink and are curled. Stir shrimp mixture into rice.

Nutritional Data

PER SERVING		EXCHANGES	
Calories:	367	Milk:	0.0
% Calories from fat:	11	Vegetable:	2.0
Fat (gm):	4.2	Fruit:	0.0
Sat. fat (gm):	0.8	Bread:	3.0
Cholesterol (mg):	175	Meat:	2.0
Sodium (mg):	237	Fat:	0.0
Protein (gm):	24.8		
Carbohydrate (gm):	54.9		

8
VEGETARIAN AND VEGETABLE DISHES

Stuffed Artichoke Casserole

Italian Bean Pot

Spinach-Peppers Tart

Herbed Ricotta-Spinach Dumplings

Vegetable Frittata with Sun-Dried Tomatoes

Vegetarian Lasagne

Eggplant Parmesan

Chick Peas and Roasted Peppers Over Polenta

Microwave Risotto and Peas

Risotto with Celery and Roasted Peppers

STUFFED ARTICHOKE CASSEROLE

We've enjoyed stuffed artichokes in Italian restaurants from New York to California. This casserole, which makes a nice side dish, recreates the flavor combinations with far less work.

5 Servings

1 14³/₄-oz. jar artichoke hearts, drained
1 tablespoon olive oil
1 large onion, chopped
1 large garlic clove, minced
²/₃ cup fat-free, reduced-sodium chicken broth, *or* regular defatted chicken broth, divided
¹/₂ teaspoon dried oregano leaves
¹/₄ teaspoon salt (optional)
¹/₈ teaspoon black pepper
2¹/₂ cups *seasoned* commercial cube-style stuffing mix

1. Preheat oven to 375 degrees. Remove and discard any tough outer leaves from artichokes. Cut artichokes into small slices.

2. In a 2¹/₂-quart oven-proof, microwave-proof casserole, combine oil, onions, garlic, and 3 tablespoons of broth. Cover with casserole lid, and microwave on high power 3 to 4 minutes, stirring contents halfway through microwaving, until onion is tender. Remove casserole from microwave oven. Stir in oregano, salt, if desired, and pepper. Add stuffing and remaining broth. Stir to mix well.

3. Stir in reserved artichokes, distributing evenly. Bake in oven, uncovered, 20 to 25 minutes or until casserole is heated through.

Nutritional Data

PER SERVING		EXCHANGES	
Calories:	138	Milk:	0.0
% Calories from fat:	22	Vegetable:	2.0
Fat (gm):	3.6	Fruit:	0.0
Sat. fat (gm):	0.4	Bread:	1.0
Cholesterol (mg):	0	Meat:	0.0
Sodium (mg):	325	Fat:	0.5
Protein (gm):	5.9		
Carbohydrate (gm):	23.5		

ITALIAN BEAN POT

Because this bean pot is prepared in the microwave oven, it's ready in a snap. We serve it as a side dish or a vegetarian main dish. Dried beans, which are first soaked and cooked, taste wonderful in the recipe. However, canned beans are more convenient and also work well.

8 Servings (side dish)

- 1 medium-sized onion, chopped
- 1½ cups diced zucchini
- ½ cup dry-packed sun-dried tomatoes
- 1 garlic clove, minced
- 1 tablespoon olive oil
- 1¾ cups dry white cannellini, *or* Great Northern, beans, cooked according to package directions
- 1 14½-oz. can reduced-sodium stewed tomatoes, *or* regular stewed tomatoes
- 1 8-oz. can reduced-sodium tomato sauce, *or* regular tomato sauce
- 1½ teaspoons dried basil leaves
- 1 teaspoon dried oregano leaves
- ¼ teaspoon salt, *or* to taste (optional)
- ⅛ teaspoon black pepper

1. In a 2½-quart microwave-proof casserole, combine onions, zucchini, sun-dried tomatoes, garlic, oil, and 2 tablespoons water. Cover with casserole lid or wax paper, and microwave on high power 6 or 7 minutes or until onions are tender; stop and stir once during microwaving.

2. Remove casserole from microwave oven. Remove tomatoes with a spoon. When cool enough to handle, finely chop tomatoes. Return tomatoes to casserole.

3. Add beans, stewed tomatoes, tomato sauce, basil, oregano, salt, if desired, and pepper. Cover and microwave on high power 6 or 7 minutes or until flavors are well blended; stop and stir once during microwaving.

Nutritional Data

PER SERVING		EXCHANGES	
Calories:	143	Milk:	0.0
% Calories from fat:	14	Vegetable:	2.0
Fat (gm):	2.4	Fruit:	0.0
Sat. fat (gm):	0.4	Bread:	1.0
Cholesterol (mg):	0	Meat:	0.0
Sodium (mg):	84	Fat:	0.5
Protein (gm):	8.2		
Carbohydrate (gm):	24.1		

SPINACH-PEPPERS TART

◆

Not quite a pizza and not quite a quiche, this tart with spinach, roasted red peppers, and cheese makes a great luncheon entree or an appetizer. With rapid-rise yeast and a food processor, you can prepare the pizza-like dough in a flash.

6 Servings

Crust

1 1/3–1 1/2   cups all-purpose white flour
  1   package rapid-rising yeast
  1/2   teaspoon salt
  1/2   teaspoon sugar
  1/2   cup hot water (125–130 degrees)
  2   teaspoons olive oil

Filling

  1   cup nonfat ricotta cheese
  1   cup (4 ozs.) shredded reduced-fat mozzarella cheese
  1/2   cup grated nonfat Parmesan cheese topping
  2   large egg whites
  2   teaspoons Italian seasoning
  1   garlic clove, minced
     Pinch ground nutmeg
  1/4   teaspoon salt (optional)
3–4   drops hot pepper sauce
  1   10-oz. package chopped frozen spinach, thawed
  1   7-oz. jar roasted red peppers, drained and chopped

1. *For crust:* In food processor container fitted with a steel blade, combine 1 1/3 cups flour, yeast, salt, and sugar. Pulse to mix. Combine water and oil in a saucepan. Heat mixture over medium-high heat to 125 degrees (or until it feels hot but does not burn fingertips).

2. With food processor on, gradually add water-oil mixture through feed tube. Process until dough forms a mass, 5 to 10 seconds. Then process 1 minute longer to knead. If necessary, add additional flour through feed tube, and continue processing until dough cleans sides of bowl. Remove dough from processor.

3. Press dough evenly into the bottom of a nonstick, spray-coated 9¹/₂-in. x 2-in. deep springform pan, covering bottom completely. Cover with plastic wrap, and let rest in a warm place 15 to 20 minutes.

4. *For filling:* While dough is resting, make filling. Preheat oven to 400 degrees. In a large bowl, stir together ricotta, mozzarella, Parmesan, egg whites, Italian seasoning, garlic, nutmeg, salt, if desired, and hot pepper sauce. A handful at a time, squeeze out as much water from spinach as possible. Stir spinach and peppers into cheese mixture, distributing evenly. Spoon filling over crust, distributing evenly. Press lightly into place.

5. Bake 45 to 50 minutes or until filling is browned and set. Cool 5 minutes on a wire rack. Run a knife around rim to loosen, and remove springform. Cut tart into wedges and serve.

Nutritional Data

PER SERVING		EXCHANGES	
Calories:	244	Milk:	0.0
% Calories from fat:	15	Vegetable:	2.0
Fat (gm):	4.1	Fruit:	0.0
Sat. fat (gm):	1	Bread:	2.0
Cholesterol (mg):	0	Meat:	1.0
Sodium (mg):	634	Fat:	0.0
Protein (gm):	16.4		
Carbohydrate (gm):	37.1		

HERBED RICOTTA-SPINACH DUMPLINGS

Serve these savory dumplings topped with some leftover poaching liquid or Parmesan cheese or marinara sauce.

For a vegetarian dish, substitute vegetable broth for the chicken broth.

5 Servings

     1 teaspoon olive oil, preferably extra-virgin
 1/4 cup chopped onions
     1 garlic clove, minced
     1 10-oz. package frozen spinach, thawed
 1/4 cup chopped parsley leaves
1 1/2 cups nonfat ricotta cheese
     1 large egg plus 1 large egg white
 3/4 cup fine dry unseasoned breadcrumbs, plus
       more as needed
 1/4 cup freshly grated Parmesan cheese
1 1/4 teaspoons dried basil leaves
 3/4 teaspoon dried marjoram leaves
 1/8 teaspoon white pepper
 1/8 teaspoon ground nutmeg
 1/2 cup (approx.) all-purpose white flour for shap-
       ing dumplings
     3 cups fat-free, reduced-sodium chicken broth,
       or defatted regular chicken broth

1. In a medium-sized microwave-proof bowl, combine oil, onions, and garlic. Cover with wax paper, and microwave on high power 1 1/2 minutes, stopping and stirring half way through. If onions are not soft and golden, microwave 30 to 40 seconds longer.

2. Drain spinach. Squeeze spinach by the handful to remove as much liquid as possible.

3. In a food processor bowl, combine onion mixture, spinach, and parsley. Process in on/off pulses until mixture is finely chopped. Add ricotta, egg and white, 3/4 cup breadcrumbs, cheese, basil, marjoram, pepper, and nutmeg. Process until mixture is blended and has a dough-like consistency. If mixture is too soft and sticky to shape, work in several

more tablespoons of breadcrumbs until manageable consistency is obtained.

4. Divide dough in half. Working on well-floured surface and with well-floured hands, form each portion of dough into about 10 oval-shaped dumplings. Set aside on wax paper.

5. In a large saucepan, bring chicken broth to a boil over high heat. Lower heat so it barely simmers. Add half of dumplings using a slotted spoon. Cook 5 to 7 minutes, until dumplings float to surface and are cooked through. Remove with a slotted spoon and reserve. If necessary, replenish broth by adding up to $1/4$ cup water. Repeat cooking procedure with remaining dumplings.

Nutritional Data

PER SERVING		EXCHANGES	
Calories:	239	Milk:	0.0
% Calories from fat:	16	Vegetable:	1.0
Fat (gm):	4.6	Fruit:	0.0
Sat. fat (gm):	1.6	Bread:	1.5
Cholesterol (mg):	46.6	Meat:	2.0
Sodium (mg):	529	Fat:	0.0
Protein (gm):	21.3		
Carbohydrate (gm):	30.7		

VEGETABLE FRITTATA WITH SUN-DRIED TOMATOES

Use a skillet that can go from stove-top to oven for this recipe. Or, transfer the sauteed mixture from a skillet to a 9 1/2-inch deep-dish pie plate or oven-proof casserole before baking.

4 Servings (main dish)

1 teaspoon butter, *or* non-diet, tub-style margarine
1 teaspoon olive oil, preferably extra-virgin
1 cup finely chopped onions
²/₃ cup chopped mixed green and red bell peppers
¹/₂ cup chopped broccoli florets
1 large garlic clove, minced
1 cup vegetable broth, *or* defatted reduced-sodium chicken broth
1¹/₄ cups finely diced, peeled all-purpose potatoes
2 whole eggs plus 4 egg whites
¹/₄ cup skim milk
3 tablespoons finely chopped oil-packed sun-dried tomatoes
1¹/₂ tablespoons pitted and finely chopped oil-cured black olives, *or* kalamata olives
3 tablespoons freshly grated Parmesan cheese, divided
³/₄ teaspoon marjoram leaves
¹/₈ teaspoon black pepper, *or* to taste

1. Preheat oven to 350 degrees. In a 10-inch nonstick skillet over medium-high heat, combine butter, oil, onions, bell peppers, broccoli, and garlic. Cook, stirring frequently, until onions are tender, about 5 minutes. Stir in broth and potatoes. Continue cooking, stirring frequently, until potatoes are just tender and almost all liquid has evaporated from pan, 6 to 9 minutes. If skillet begins to boil dry, add a bit more broth or water as needed. Remove skillet from heat. Spread vegetable mixture in skillet (or transfer to pie plate).

2. In a medium-sized bowl, beat together eggs and whites, milk, tomatoes, olives, half of cheese, marjoram, and pepper. Pour mixture over vegetables. Sprinkle remaining cheese over top.

3. Bake in center third of oven 10 minutes. Lower heat to 325 degrees, and bake 10 to 18 minutes longer or until fritatta is barely set in center when dish is jiggled. (Time will vary greatly depending on pan used.)

4. Transfer to a cooling rack. Let stand for 5 minutes. Immediately cut into wedges and serve, using a wide-bladed spatula. Fritatta may also be refrigerated, then reheated in a low oven or in a microwave oven on 50 percent power.

Nutritional Data

PER SERVING		EXCHANGES	
Calories:	223	Milk:	0.0
% Calories from fat:	32	Vegetable:	1.0
Fat (gm):	8.1	Fruit:	0.0
Sat. fat (gm):	2.7	Bread:	1.5
Cholesterol (mg):	113	Meat:	1.0
Sodium (mg):	339	Fat:	1.0
Protein (gm):	12.1		
Carbohydrate (gm):	26.4		

VEGETARIAN LASAGNE

◆

*If you're cooking a meal for both vegetarians and non-vegetarians
and don't want to fix two different main dishes, this hearty
vegetable lasagne is a perfect choice. Offer a meat sauce
(see page 42) along with the lasagne so those who wish
can serve themselves some.*

*The microwave oven speeds preparation of this dish.
We also cut preparation time by relying on ready-to-use
frozen bell peppers and onions.*

6 Servings

12 ozs. uncooked lasagne noodles
2 cups thinly sliced zucchini
1 16-oz. bag frozen mixed red, green, and yellow
   bell peppers with onions
2 garlic cloves, minced
2 teaspoons olive oil
3 15-oz. cans reduced-sodium tomato sauce, *or*
   regular tomato sauce
1 tablespoon plus 1 teaspoon Italian seasoning
1/4 teaspoon salt (optional)
   Pinch of black pepper
6 ozs. (1 1/2 cups loosely packed) shredded
   reduced-fat mozzarella cheese, divided
4 ozs. (1 cup loosely packed) shredded nonfat
   mozzarella cheese
1 15-oz. carton nonfat ricotta cheese
1/2 cup (2 ozs.) grated nonfat Parmesan cheese
   topping, divided

1. Preheat oven to 375 degrees. Coat a 9 1/2-in. x 13-in. baking pan with cooking spray. Cook noodles according to package directions. Rinse and drain in a colander.

2. Meanwhile, in an 8-cup measure or similar microwave-proof bowl, combine zucchini, peppers and onions, garlic, and oil. Cover with wax paper, and microwave on high power 6 minutes or until onions are tender; stir once during microwaving. Remove from microwave and add tomato sauce, Italian seasoning, salt, if desired, and pepper. Stir to mix well.

3. Reserve ¼ cup reduced-fat mozzarella. Mix together ricotta and remaining mozzarella cheeses.

4. Arrange a one-noodle-thick layer of lasagne noodles in bottom of prepared pan, overlapping slightly. Top noodles with ½ of ricotta-mozzarella mixture, spreading it out evenly. Sprinkle ⅓ of the Parmesan evenly over ricotta mixture. Add ⅓ of sauce, spreading evenly. Top with another layer of noodles, another ½ of ricotta-mozzarella mixture, and another ⅓ of Parmesan. Top with a layer of sauce. Finish with last of noodles and then last of sauce, arranging zucchini slices attractively on lasagne top. Reserve remaining ⅓ of Parmesan and ¼ cup of reduced-fat mozzarella.

5. Bake in preheated oven 40 to 45 minutes or until lasagne sauce is bubbly. Sprinkle with remaining mozzarella and Parmesan cheeses, and bake an additional 2 minutes until cheese is partially melted. Let stand 5 minutes before cutting into 6 or 8 portions.

Note: Lasagne can be made one or two days ahead, covered, and refrigerated until reheated and served.

Nutritional Data

PER SERVING		EXCHANGES	
Calories:	417	Milk:	0.0
% Calories from fat:	15	Vegetable:	5.0
Fat (gm):	7.2	Fruit:	0.0
Sat. fat (gm):	1.3	Bread:	2.5
Cholesterol (mg):	0	Meat:	2.0
Sodium (mg):	501	Fat:	0.0
Protein (gm):	31.7		
Carbohydrate (gm):	60.7		

EGGPLANT PARMESAN

Although the eggplant slices are fried in most versions of this Italian classic, baking is easier, healthier, and yields equally tasty results. If time is short, a good-quality meatless commercial pasta sauce may be substituted for one of our homemade pasta sauces (see Chapter 4).

9 Servings

- 1 cup fine, dry breadcrumbs
- 1/4 cup plus 1 tablespoon freshly grated Parmesan cheese, divided
- 1/4 teaspoon black pepper
- 2 medium-sized eggplants (about 2 1/4 lbs. total), peeled and cut crosswise into 1/2-in. slices
- 2 egg whites beaten with 2 tablespoons water, *or* 2/3 cup liquid egg substitute
- 3 cups Tomatoes and Peppers Sauce (p. 47), Marinara Sauce, (p. 45), *or* meatless commercial pasta sauce
- 1 cup (4 ozs.) shredded reduced-fat mozzarella cheese

1. Preheat oven to 475 degrees. Coat a 12-in. x 18-in. baking sheet with cooking spray. Also spray a 3-quart flat, rectangular casserole or lasagne pan with cooking spray.

2. In a large, shallow bowl, stir together breadcrumbs, 1/4 cup Parmesan, and pepper until well mixed. In another bowl, set out egg white mixture. One at a time, dip eggplant slices into egg white mixture, shaking off any excess. Then dip each eggplant slice into breadcrumb mixture until evenly coated. Arrange slices, separated, on baking sheet.

3. Bake in upper third of oven until slices are nicely browned, about 10 to 12 minutes. Turn over using a spatula. Return to oven; bake slices 8 to 10 minutes longer or until well browned. Set aside.

4. Spread about half of pasta sauce in prepared casserole. Using a spatula, transfer eggplant to casserole, overlapping slices slightly. Top with remaining pasta sauce, then mozzarella. Sprinkle with remaining 1 tablespoon Parmesan.

5. Reset oven to 375 degrees. Bake until sauce is bubbly, about 15 minutes longer.

Nutritional Data

PER SERVING		EXCHANGES	
Calories:	216	Milk:	0.0
% Calories from fat:	30	Vegetable:	3.0
Fat (gm):	7.6	Fruit:	0.0
Sat. fat (gm):	2.6	Bread:	1.0
Cholesterol (mg):	9.8	Meat:	0.5
Sodium (mg):	290	Fat:	1.0
Protein (gm):	10.2		
Carbohydrate (gm):	30.2		

CHICK PEAS AND ROASTED PEPPERS OVER POLENTA

Polenta started out as peasant fare but has made its way into many up-scale restaurants. It makes a nice change from pasta. We've simplified the preparation of this vegetarian entree considerably by preparing the polenta in the microwave while the vegetables are cooking. For an even more streamlined version, serve over cooked rice.

5 Servings

Vegetables and Sauce

    1 medium-sized onion, chopped
    1 garlic clove, minced
    2 teaspoons olive oil
    1 15-oz. can chick peas, well rinsed and drained
    1 15-oz. can reduced-sodium tomato sauce, *or* regular tomato sauce
    1 14$\frac{1}{2}$-oz. can reduced-sodium stewed tomatoes, *or* regular stewed tomatoes
    1 7-oz. jar roasted red peppers, drained and chopped
    1 medium zucchini, chopped
    1 teaspoon Italian seasoning
    $\frac{1}{8}$ teaspoon salt, *or* to taste (optional)
    $\frac{1}{8}$ teaspoon black pepper

Polenta

    1$\frac{1}{3}$ cups yellow cornmeal

1 tablespoon granulated sugar
$^1/_2$ teaspoon salt, *or* to taste (optional)
$3^1/_4$ cups water
1 cup 1% fat milk
1 medium-sized onion, diced
$^1/_4$ cup (1 oz.) grated nonfat Parmesan cheese topping

1. *For vegetables and sauce:* In a large saucepan, combine onions, garlic, and oil. Cook over medium heat, stirring frequently, until onions have softened, 3 to 4 minutes. If vegetables begin to stick, add a bit of water. Add chick peas, tomato sauce, and stewed tomatoes. Add roasted peppers, zucchini, Italian seasoning, salt, if desired, and black pepper. Stir to mix well. Bring to a boil. Reduce heat, cover, and simmer 15 to 18 minutes until flavors are well blended. Keep warm until polenta is ready.

2. *For polenta:* While vegetables and sauce are cooking, make polenta. In a 3-quart microwave-proof casserole, combine cornmeal, sugar, salt, if desired, water, milk, and onions. Stir to mix well. Microwave, uncovered, on high power 8 to 9 minutes; stop and stir with a wire whisk after 3 minutes and 6 minutes. Stir again with a wire whisk until mixture is smooth. Whisk in cheese. Cover with casserole top and cook an additional 4 to 5 minutes on high power.

3. Remove from microwave oven, and let stand an additional 2 or 3 minutes. Serve chick pea mixture over polenta.

Nutritional Data

PER SERVING		EXCHANGES	
Calories:	352	Milk:	0.0
% Calories from fat:	13	Vegetable:	4.0
Fat (gm):	5.3	Fruit:	0.0
Sat. fat (gm):	1	Bread:	3.0
Cholesterol (mg):	2	Meat:	0.0
Sodium (mg):	689	Fat:	1.0
Protein (gm):	13.7		
Carbohydrate (gm):	64.8		

MICROWAVE RISOTTO AND PEAS

◆

*Peas and rice are often served together in Venice—but with
far more fat than is used in this slimmed down version. (We've
substituted nonfat Parmesan cheese for some of the butter.)
The microwave makes preparation quick and easy. Incidentally,
this casserole is hearty enough for a vegetable main dish.*

6 Servings (side dish)

Risotto

- ³/₄ cup uncooked arborio rice
- 2 teaspoons olive oil
- 2 teaspoons butter, *or* margarine
- 2²/₃ cups fat-free, reduced-sodium chicken broth,
  or regular defatted chicken broth
- ¹/₄ teaspoon dried thyme leaves
- ¹/₈ teaspoon black pepper

Peas

- 1 small onion, chopped
- 1 small garlic clove, minced
- 1 cup fat-free, reduced-sodium chicken broth, *or*
  regular defatted chicken broth, divided
- 2 cups frozen green peas
- 2 tablespoons chopped parsley leaves
- ¹/₂ cup grated nonfat Parmesan cheese topping
  Salt, to taste

1. *For risotto:* In a 2¹/₂-quart microwave-proof casserole, combine rice, oil, and butter. Microwave, uncovered, 60 seconds on high power. Stir well. Add broth, thyme, and pepper. Stir to mix well. Cover with casserole lid, and microwave on high power 7 to 8 minutes. Stir well. Uncover and microwave an additional 11 to 13 minutes or until most of liquid is absorbed and rice is tender. Allow to stand 2 to 3 minutes.

2. *For peas:* While risotto is cooking, in a large saucepan, combine onions, garlic, and 2 tablespoons of broth. Cook over medium heat, stirring frequently, until onions are tender, 5 or 6 minutes. Add remaining broth, peas, and parsley. Bring to a boil. Reduce heat, and simmer until peas are cooked, 5 or 6 minutes.

3. Stir peas into the risotto. Stir in Parmesan. Add salt, if desired. Garnish with parsley sprigs, if desired.

Nutritional Data

PER SERVING		EXCHANGES	
Calories:	206	Milk:	0.0
% Calories from fat:	16	Vegetable:	0.0
Fat (gm):	3.6	Fruit:	0.0
Sat. fat (gm):	1	Bread:	2.0
Cholesterol (mg):	3.4	Meat:	0.5
Sodium (mg):	326	Fat:	0.5
Protein (gm):	10		
Carbohydrate (gm):	31.5		

RISOTTO WITH CELERY AND ROASTED PEPPERS

The rice used in risotto, called arborio rice, has short, rounded grains and a translucent appearance. It is very absorbent and starchy, which accounts for its creamy, almost pudding-like consistency. Arborio rice is sold in gourmet shops, the gourmet sections of some supermarkets, Italian markets, and by mail order firms. If necessary, you can substitute granza or paella rice, a somewhat similar short-grained rice sold in ethnic Spanish markets. American short-grained rice, on the other hand, will not yield satisfactory results.

Unlike many risottos, this colorful and tempting Venetian-style version doesn't need constant stirring during cooking. It makes a light, meatless entree or a savory accompaniment for all sorts of main dishes.

5 Servings

2 teaspoons olive oil, preferably extra-virgin
2 teaspoons unsalted butter, *or* margarine
3/4 cup finely chopped onions
2 large garlic cloves, minced
2 1/2 cups diced celery
2 3/4–3 1/2 cups fat-free, reduced-sodium chicken broth, *or* vegetable broth
3/4 cup arborio rice
1 11-oz. jar roasted red sweet peppers, drained and chopped
1/8 teaspoon hot red pepper flakes
1/4 cup freshly grated Parmesan cheese
3 tablespoons tomato sauce

1. In a medium-sized saucepan over medium-high heat, stir together olive oil, butter, onions, garlic, and celery. Cook, stirring, 7 or 8 minutes or until onions are translucent and beginning to brown.

2. Add 2 3/4 cups broth; let come to a boil. Stir in rice, roasted sweet peppers, and hot pepper flakes. Adjust heat so mixture simmers gently. Cook, stirring occasionally, until rice is barely tender, 18 to 22 minutes.

Add more broth if mixture begins to thicken; it should remain slightly soupy.

3. Stir in Parmesan and tomato sauce until well blended, and serve.

Nutritional Data

PER SERVING		EXCHANGES	
Calories:	225	Milk:	0.0
% Calories from fat:	21	Vegetable:	1.0
Fat (gm):	5.2	Fruit:	0.0
Sat. fat (gm):	2.3	Bread:	2.0
Cholesterol (mg):	8.4	Meat:	0.0
Sodium (mg):	764	Fat:	1.0
Protein (gm):	8.7		
Carbohydrate (gm):	35.5		

9
VEGETABLE
SIDE DISHES

Roasted Vegetables

Crumb-Topped Tomato-Gremolata Bake

Peperonata

Chunky Caponata

Zucchini-Mushroom Saute

Pan-Grilled Vegetables

Eggplant Skillet with Parsley

Braised Escarole

Braised Broccoli with Garlic Breadcrumbs

Lemon-Parmesan Asparagus

ROASTED VEGETABLES

◆

*This is one of our favorite winter side dishes. Nonfat
Parmesan helps give the vegetables a crisp texture and rich
flavor. Microwaving the root vegetables before baking them
speeds the cooking time considerably.*

4 Servings

    4 medium-sized onions, cut into large chunks
1½ lbs. (4½ cups) thin-skinned potatoes, cut into
        2-in. pieces
    2 cups baby carrots, *or* 2 cups peeled and thickly
        sliced regular carrots
    1 large zucchini, sliced
1½ tablespoons olive oil
    1 garlic clove, minced
    2 teaspoons Italian seasoning
¼ teaspoon salt, *or* to taste (optional)
⅛ teaspoon black pepper
⅓ cup grated nonfat Parmesan cheese topping

1. Preheat oven to 450 degrees. Combine onions, potatoes, and carrots in
   an 8-cup measure or similar bowl. Add 2 tablespoons water. Cover
   with wax paper, and microwave on high power 8 to 10 minutes or until
   vegetables are partially cooked, stopping and stirring once.

2. Meanwhile, cut zucchini in half lengthwise, then crosswise into 1-inch
   slices. Set aside until needed.

3. Transfer potato mixture to a large nonstick baking pan or rimmed baking sheet lightly coated with cooking spray. Drizzle with oil. Sprinkle
   with garlic, Italian seasoning, salt, if desired, and pepper. Stir to mix
   well.

4. Bake in preheated oven, stirring occasionally, 20 minutes or until vegetables begin to brown and are almost tender. Stir zucchini into vegetable mixture. Sprinkle with Parmesan, and stir to mix well. Bake an
   additional 10 minutes.

Nutritional Data

PER SERVING		EXCHANGES	
Calories:	310	Milk:	0.0
% Calories from fat:	16	Vegetable:	3.0
Fat (gm):	5.6	Fruit:	0.0
Sat. fat (gm):	0.8	Bread:	2.5
Cholesterol (mg):	0	Meat:	0.0
Sodium (mg):	98	Fat:	1.0
Protein (gm):	9		
Carbohydrate (gm):	59		

CRUMB-TOPPED TOMATO-GREMOLATA BAKE

An Italian seasoning mixture often sprinkled on vegetables, poultry, and seafood, gremolata usually features chopped fresh herbs—particularly parsley and garlic—and grated lemon zest.

Here, a sprightly, minty gremolata and a crispy breadcrumb-and-Parmesan topping make a succulent addition to baked tomato halves. (Be sure to use vine-ripened tomatoes in this recipe.) This is a good side dish to serve with grilled or roasted meats.

6 Servings

   3 large vine-ripened tomatoes, cored, and halved vertically
$1/8$ teaspoon salt (optional)
   1 teaspoon olive oil, preferably extra-virgin
   2 large garlic cloves, minced
$1/4$ cup finely chopped parsley leaves
   2 tablespoons finely chopped fresh mint leaves
$1/2$ teaspoon finely grated lemon zest (yellow part of peel)
$1/8$ teaspoon black pepper
$1/4$ cup fine dry breadcrumbs
$1 1/2$ tablespoons freshly grated Parmesan cheese

1. Preheat oven to 425 degrees. Set tomato halves, cut side up, in a flat oven-proof dish large enough to hold them. Sprinkle salt over halves, if desired.

2. *For gremolata:* In a small bowl, stir together oil, garlic, parsley, mint, lemon zest, and pepper. Sprinkle gremolata over tomato halves, dividing it equally among them. Bake tomatoes on upper oven rack for 10 minutes.

3. *For crumb topping:* Meanwhile, in the bowl used for the gremolata, stir together breadcrumbs and Parmesan. Sprinkle over the partially baked tomatoes, dividing it equally among them. Bake 6 to 9 minutes longer, until topping is golden brown and crispy. Remove dish from oven; let stand at least 5 minutes. Tomatoes may be served right away or held for several hours. Reheat to hot before serving.

Nutritional Data

PER SERVING		EXCHANGES	
Calories:	48	Milk:	0.0
% Calories from fat:	31	Vegetable:	1.0
Fat (gm):	1.7	Fruit:	0.0
Sat. fat (gm):	0.5	Bread:	0.0
Cholesterol (mg):	1.2	Meat:	0.0
Sodium (mg):	75	Fat:	0.5
Protein (gm):	1.9		
Carbohydrate (gm):	6.8		

PEPERONATA

◆

Peperonata is a spicy, colorful side dish featuring an abundance of sweet (bell) peppers. Often served at room temperature like a relish, it is particularly good with grilled meats.

5 Servings

 1 tablespoon olive oil, preferably extra-virgin
 2 large onions, cut lengthwise into thin shreds
 1 large garlic clove, minced
 4 cups 2-in.-long strips of mixed green and red bell peppers
 1 14½-oz. can reduced-sodium Italian-style chopped tomatoes, including juice, *or* regular Italian-style chopped tomatoes, including juice
 1 tablespoon tomato paste
 1 teaspoon granulated sugar
 ⅛ teaspoon black pepper, *or* to taste
   Pinch of hot red pepper flakes (optional)
 2 teaspoons balsamic vinegar
 1 tablespoon red wine vinegar, *or* more to taste
 ¼ teaspoon salt (optional)

1. In a 12-inch nonstick skillet over high heat, combine oil, onions, garlic, and peppers. Adjust heat so onions brown but do not burn, and cook, stirring, until they are golden, 6 or 7 minutes. Stir in tomatoes, tomato paste, sugar, black pepper, and red pepper flakes.

2. Adjust heat so mixture simmers gently and cook, uncovered and stirring occasionally, 20 minutes. Add vinegars and continue simmering, stirring frequently to prevent sticking, until flavors are blended, about 10 minutes longer. Add salt, if desired.

Nutritional Data

PER SERVING		EXCHANGES	
Calories:	123	Milk:	0.0
% Calories from fat:	22	Vegetable:	4.0
Fat (gm):	3.4	Fruit:	0.0
Sat. fat (gm):	0.5	Bread:	0.0
Cholesterol (mg):	0	Meat:	0.0
Sodium (mg):	43	Fat:	0.5
Protein (gm):	3.3		
Carbohydrate (gm):	23.2		

CHUNKY CAPONATA

*Normally, eggplant acts like a blotter and soaks up a lot
of oil during sauteing. However, partially cooking it in a
microwave oven changes the consistency so it can be sauteed
like other vegetables with just a little fat.*

*Unlike many caponatas, which are smooth enough to use
as dips and spreads, this one has a chunky, stew-like
consistency and is served as a side dish.*

6 Servings

- 1 medium-sized eggplant (1 lb.), peeled and cut into $3/4$-in. chunks
- 1 tablespoon olive oil, preferably extra-virgin
- 2 medium-sized onions, coarsely chopped
- 2 medium-sized bell peppers, preferably one red and one green, seeded and cut into $3/4$-in. chunks
- 2 large garlic cloves, minced
- 4 cups $3/4$-in. zucchini chunks
- $1/2$ cup chopped parsley leaves
- 1 $14^1/2$-oz. can reduced-sodium Italian-style tomatoes, with juice, *or* regular Italian-style tomatoes, with juice
- $1/4$ cup tomato paste
- $3/4$ cup vegetable broth, *or* water
- 1 teaspoon granulated sugar
- $3/4$ teaspoon dried marjoram leaves
- $1/4$ teaspoon black pepper, *or* to taste
- $1/4$ teaspoon salt (optional)

1. Spread eggplant on a microwave-proof plate. Sprinkle with 2 tablespoons water. Cover with wax paper. Microwave on high power 2 minutes. Stir to redistribute eggplant. Re-cover and microwave 1 to 2 minutes longer or until pieces are just tender when pierced with a fork. Drain off all liquid. Pat dry with paper towels.

2. In a 12-inch, deep-sided, nonstick saute pan or 4-quart pot over medium-high heat, combine oil, onions, bell peppers, and garlic. Cook, stirring, about 5 minutes or until onions are limp and beginning to brown. Add zucchini, parsley, and eggplant to skillet. Cook,

stirring frequently, 5 minutes longer. Coarsely chop tomatoes and add them and their juice to pan.

3. In a small bowl, stir together tomato paste, vegetable broth, sugar, marjoram, and black pepper until well blended. Stir tomato paste mixture into pan. Adjust heat so mixture simmers gently. Cook, uncovered, stirring occasionally, 20 to 25 minutes or until vegetables are tender and flavors well blended. Stir in salt, if desired.

Nutritional Data

PER SERVING		EXCHANGES	
Calories:	121	Milk:	0.0
% Calories from fat:	20	Vegetable:	4.0
Fat (gm):	3.1	Fruit:	0.0
Sat. fat (gm):	0.4	Bread:	0.0
Cholesterol (mg):	0	Meat:	0.0
Sodium (mg):	116	Fat:	0.5
Protein (gm):	4.1		
Carbohydrate (gm):	23		

ZUCCHINI-MUSHROOM SAUTE

A light, mildly flavored side dish, this goes well with a wide variety of hearty Italian entrees.

5 Servings

- 1½ teaspoons olive oil, preferably extra-virgin
- 1 small onion, chopped
- 1½ cups coarsely sliced mushrooms
- 1 large garlic clove, minced
- 4 medium-sized (6½ in.) zucchini, cut into ½-in. cubes
- ¼ cup fat-free, reduced-sodium chicken broth, *or* vegetable broth
- 1 tablespoon finely chopped fresh basil, *or* ½ teaspoon dried basil leaves
- ¼ teaspoon salt, *or* to taste (optional)
- ⅛ teaspoon black pepper, *or* to taste
  Pinch of hot red pepper flakes (optional)

1. In a 12-inch nonstick skillet over high heat, heat oil until hot, but not smoking. Add onions and mushrooms. Adjust heat so mixture cooks rapidly but does not burn, and cook, stirring, 3 minutes. Add garlic; continue cooking until mushrooms are nicely browned, about 3 minutes longer.

2. Stir in zucchini, broth, basil, salt, if desired, pepper, and hot pepper flakes, if desired. Cook, stirring frequently, until zucchini pieces are just tender, 6 to 9 minutes longer.

Nutritional Data

PER SERVING		EXCHANGES	
Calories:	40	Milk:	0.0
% Calories from fat:	32	Vegetable:	1.0
Fat (gm):	1.6	Fruit:	0.0
Sat. fat (gm):	0.2	Bread:	0.0
Cholesterol (mg):	0	Meat:	0.0
Sodium (mg):	21	Fat:	0.5
Protein (gm):	2.1		
Carbohydrate (gm):	5.7		

PAN-GRILLED VEGETABLES

◆

Here's a quick-and-easy vegetable skillet that makes a nice accompaniment to our Turkey with Lemon-Caper Sauce (page 98).

4 Servings

1½ teaspoons olive oil
1 large onion, sliced
1 garlic clove, minced
1 large red, *or* green, bell pepper, seeded and cut into strips
1 large zucchini, sliced, *or* 2 cups sliced cauliflower florets
½ teaspoon dried thyme leaves
¼ teaspoon salt, *or* to taste (optional)
⅛ teaspoon black pepper

1. In a 12-inch nonstick skillet over medium-high heat, warm oil until hot, but not smoking. Add onions, garlic, bell peppers, and zucchini (or cauliflower). Sprinkle vegetables with thyme, salt, if desired, and black pepper.

2. Adjust heat so mixture cooks rapidly but does not burn. Cook, stirring frequently and breaking onion slices into rings, until vegetable slices are nicely browned and begin to char slightly, 8 to 10 minutes.

Nutritional Data

PER SERVING		EXCHANGES	
Calories:	56	Milk:	0.0
% Calories from fat:	29	Vegetable:	1.5
Fat (gm):	2	Fruit:	0.0
Sat. fat (gm):	0.3	Bread:	0.0
Cholesterol (mg):	0	Meat:	0.0
Sodium (mg):	2	Fat:	0.5
Protein (gm):	1.8		
Carbohydrate (gm):	9.2		

EGGPLANT SKILLET WITH PARSLEY

◊

Although preparation and ingredients are simple, this is a surprisingly savory dish. As is the case in several other recipes in this cookbook, we call for quickly microwaving the eggplant pieces before sauteing them. This makes it possible to cook with far less oil than would otherwise be needed.

4 Servings

    2 small eggplants (about 1¾ lbs.) peeled and cut
      into ¾-in. cubes
    2 teaspoons olive oil, preferably extra-virgin
    1 small onion, finely chopped
    1 large garlic clove, minced
   ¼ cup chopped fresh parsley leaves
    1 tablespoon chopped fresh basil leaves, *or* 1
      teaspoon dried basil leaves
   ¼ teaspoon black pepper, *or* to taste
¼–½ teaspoon salt (optional)
    1 teaspoon fresh lemon juice combined with 2
      teaspoons water

1. Spread eggplant in a large microwave-proof pie plate or plate. Sprinkle a tablespoon of water over eggplant. Cover with wax paper. Microwave on high power 3 to 4 minutes, stirring after 2 minutes, until pieces are barely tender when tested with a fork. Turn out into a colander and drain well. Pat dry with paper towels.

2. In a 12-inch or larger nonstick saute pan or skillet, heat oil to hot, but not smoking, over high heat. Add eggplant, onions, and garlic. Adjust heat so mixture browns but does not burn, and cook, stirring, until pieces are nicely browned and tender. Stir in parsley, basil, pepper, salt, if desired, and lemon juice-water mixture. Cook several minutes longer, until piping hot.

Nutritional Data

PER SERVING		EXCHANGES	
Calories:	82	Milk:	0.0
% Calories from fat:	27	Vegetable:	2.5
Fat (gm):	2.7	Fruit:	0.0
Sat. fat (gm):	0.4	Bread:	0.0
Cholesterol (mg):	0	Meat:	0.0
Sodium (mg):	9	Fat:	0.5
Protein (gm):	2		
Carbohydrate (gm):	14.8		

BRAISED ESCAROLE

Cooked and raw escarole look and taste so different they don't even seem like the same vegetable! As is also true with curly endive and Belgian endive, braising mellows the bitterness and lends the escarole a distinctive "cooked greens" taste. The addition of chopped black olives and raisins is a traditonal Italian touch.

4 Servings

2 small heads escarole
1/2 teaspoon olive oil
2 large garlic cloves, minced
1/2 cup fat-free, reduced-sodium chicken broth, *or* defatted regular chicken broth
3 tablespoons chopped dark raisins
1 tablespoon chopped oil-cured black olives, *or* kalamata black olives
1/8 teaspoon black pepper, *or* to taste
1/2 teaspoon butter, *or* non-diet, tub-style margarine

1. Thoroughly wash and drain escarole heads. Leaving enough of the core to hold each escarole head intact, trim off brown area of root ends. Pull off and discard bitter or tough outer leaves so only pale, tender, green leaves remain. Cut each head in half lengthwise. Handling gently to keep each portion intact, pat dry with paper towels.

2. Heat oil over medium-high heat in a 4- to 5-quart pot. Add garlic, and cook several minutes until it is fragrant. Add broth, raisins, olives, and pepper. Bring mixture to a boil. Adjust mixture so it boils briskly, and cook until liquid almost completely evaporates from pot, about 5 minutes.

3. Lay escarole in pot. Cover and simmer, gently turning leaves once or twice, until escarole is tender, 10 to 12 minutes. Add butter; heat until melted. Serve escarole with pot liquid and raisin-olive mixture spooned over top.

Nutritional Data

PER SERVING		EXCHANGES	
Calories:	46	Milk:	0.0
% Calories from fat:	34	Vegetable:	1.0
Fat (gm):	1.9	Fruit:	0.0
Sat. fat (gm):	0.5	Bread:	0.0
Cholesterol (mg):	1.3	Meat:	0.0
Sodium (mg):	123	Fat:	0.5
Protein (gm):	1.3		
Carbohydrate (gm):	7.1		

BRAISED BROCCOLI WITH GARLIC BREADCRUMBS

Toasted, garlic-infused breadcrumbs add an appealing crunch to this dish. It should be served immediately, as the crumbs lose their crispness and broccoli its bright color upon standing.

4 Servings

- 1½ teaspoons olive oil, preferably extra-virgin, divided
- 2 large garlic cloves, peeled and smashed
- 3 tablespoons fine dry breadcrumbs
- ¼ teaspoon dried oregano leaves
- ⅔ cup vegetable broth, *or* defatted reduced-sodium chicken broth
- 4 cups broccoli florets
- 1 teaspoon fresh lemon juice combined with 1 teaspoon water
- ¼ teaspoon black pepper, *or* to taste
- ¼ teaspoon salt (optional)

1. In a 12-inch or larger nonstick saute pan or skillet, heat 1 teaspoon of oil and garlic over medium-high heat. Adjust heat so garlic does not brown or burn and cook several minutes, pressing on garlic to express as much juice as possible. Discard garlic.

2. Add breadcrumbs; continue cooking, stirring, several minutes until crumbs are nicely browned and oil is distributed throughout. Stir oregano into breadcrumbs. Remove crumbs from pan and reserve.

3. Bring broth to a boil over medium-high heat in pan previously used. Add broccoli and simmer, stirring occasionally, until most liquid has evaporated and broccoli is crisp tender, about 5 minutes. Stir in lemon juice-water mixture, pepper, salt, if desired, and remaining olive oil. Stir until broccoli is coated. Sprinkle crumbs over broccoli and serve.

Nutritional Data

PER SERVING		EXCHANGES	
Calories:	68	Milk:	0.0
% Calories from fat:	27	Vegetable:	2.0
Fat (gm):	2.3	Fruit:	0.0
Sat. fat (gm):	0.3	Bread:	0.0
Cholesterol (mg):	0	Meat:	0.0
Sodium (mg):	81	Fat:	0.5
Protein (gm):	3.5		
Carbohydrate (gm):	10.3		

LEMON-PARMESAN ASPARAGUS

We love to serve this side dish in spring and early summer when the new crop of asparagus appears. In winter you could substitute two 10-ounce packages of frozen asparagus, cooked according to directions.

8 Servings

- 2 lbs. fresh, untrimmed asparagus spears
- 1/4 cup (1 oz.) grated nonfat Parmesan cheese topping
- 1/4 cup fat-free, reduced-sodium chicken broth, *or* regular defatted chicken broth
- 2 teaspoons olive oil
- 2 teaspoons lemon juice
- 1/4 teaspoon dry mustard
- 1/8 teaspoon salt (optional)
- 2–3 drops hot pepper sauce
- 1 tablespoon breadcrumbs made from fresh bread

1. Wash asparagus well. Gently break off and discard tough white part at bottom of each spear. Lay spears in a large skillet and cover with water. Cover skillet and bring water to a boil over high heat. Reduce heat and simmer 3 to 7 minutes or until spears are crisp-tender.

2. While asparagus is cooking, in a small bowl, mix together Parmesan, broth, oil, lemon juice, mustard, salt, if desired, and hot pepper sauce.

3. Transfer asparagus to a colander and drain well. Arrange on a serving platter. Drizzle Parmesan mixture over asparagus. Sprinkle with bread-crumbs and serve immediately.

Nutritional Data

PER SERVING		EXCHANGES	
Calories:	45	Milk:	0.0
% Calories from fat:	26	Vegetable:	1.0
Fat (gm):	1.5	Fruit:	0.0
Sat. fat (gm):	0.2	Bread:	0.0
Cholesterol (mg):	0	Meat:	0.0
Sodium (mg):	47	Fat:	0.5
Protein (gm):	3.9		
Carbohydrate (gm):	5.8		

10
BREADS AND PIZZAS

Basic Pizza Crust

Pizza with Caramelized Onions and Smoked Turkey

Artichoke and Olive Pizza

Pepperoni Pizza

Calzone Dough

Spinach Calzone

Sausage and Peppers Calzone

Focaccia with Onions and Sun-Dried Tomatoes

Sesame Breadsticks

BASIC PIZZA CRUST

♦

Fresh, homemade dough makes a real difference in the taste of a pizza. If you have a bread machine, you probably already have a much-used recipe. If not, try this quick and easy one. It's made with a food processor and features rapid-rising yeast.

4 Servings (makes 13-in. diameter or 10x14-in. rectangular crust)

- 1³/₄–2 cups all-purpose white flour
- 1 package rapid-rising yeast
- ¹/₂–³/₄ teaspoon salt
- ¹/₂ teaspoon sugar
- ²/₃ cup water (125–130 degrees)
- 1 tablespoon olive oil

1. In food processor container fitted with a steel blade, combine 1³/₄ cups flour, yeast, salt, and sugar. Pulse to mix.

2. Combine hot water and oil in a saucepan. Heat mixture over medium-high heat to 125 degrees (or until it feels hot but does not burn finger-tips). With food processor on, gradually add water-oil mixture through feed tube. Process until dough forms a mass, 5 to 10 seconds. Then process 1 minute longer to knead. If necessary, add additional flour through feed tube and continue processing until dough cleans sides of bowl. Remove dough from processor, and shape into a ball.

3. Turn dough out into a shallow bowl coated with cooking spray. Turn dough once to coat with spray. Cover with plastic wrap, and let rise 15 minutes.

4. Transfer dough to a pizza pan or baking sheet coated with nonstick spray and lightly dusted with cornmeal, if desired. Stretch and shape dough by hand or with rolling pin into a 12- or 13-inch circle or 11- or 14-inch rectangle.

5. Complete pizza with desired sauce, cheese, and toppings. Bake according to directions in following pizza recipes.

Nutritional Data

PER SERVING		EXCHANGES	
Calories:	236	Milk:	0.0
% Calories from fat:	13	Vegetable:	0.0
Fat (gm):	3.9	Fruit:	0.0
Sat. fat (gm):	0.5	Bread:	3.0
Cholesterol (mg):	0	Meat:	0.0
Sodium (mg):	268	Fat:	0.5
Protein (gm):	6.4		
Carbohydrate (gm):	43		

PIZZA WITH CARAMELIZED ONIONS AND SMOKED TURKEY

Caramelized onions and smoked turkey make a wonderful pizza topping—and our recipe caramelizes the onions with very little fat. If you like, substitute a ready-made crust for our homemade one.

Incidentally, if you've traveled in Italy, you've noticed that many pizzerias make their pizzas in large sheets and sell individual portions in rectangles. So feel free to shape dough into a rectangle rather than a round; it's just as authentic.

4 Servings

- 1 tablespoon butter
- 2 cups thinly sliced onions
- 1/2 tablespoon sugar
- 3 ozs. reduced-sodium, low-fat deli smoked turkey, cut into thin strips
- 1 Basic Pizza Crust (page 156)
- 3/4 cup reduced-fat, reduced-sodium pizza sauce, *or* regular pizza sauce
- 4 ozs. (1 cup loosely packed) shredded reduced-fat mozzarella cheese

1. Preheat oven to 450 degrees. Melt butter in a 12-inch nonstick skillet over medium heat. Stir in onions and sugar. Cook, stirring frequently, until onions caramelize and turn light brown, 12 to 15 minutes. Add turkey and cook an additional minute, stirring, so that flavors blend. Remove from heat, and set aside.

2. Form pizza crust (if homemade) into a 12- or 13-inch circle or a 12 x 14-inch rectangle. Spread pizza sauce evenly over pizza crust, leaving a narrow line of crust uncoated at outer edge. Sprinkle evenly with cheese. Distribute onions and turkey mixture evenly over pizza.

3. Bake in preheated oven 15 to 17 minutes (or according to directions if a purchased crust is used) or until edges of crust are browned. Cut into 8 wedges or rectangles.

Nutritional Data

PER SERVING		EXCHANGES	
Calories:	414	Milk:	0.0
% Calories from fat:	23	Vegetable:	3.0
Fat (gm):	10.6	Fruit:	0.0
Sat. fat (gm):	3.4	Bread:	3.0
Cholesterol (mg):	16.4	Meat:	1.0
Sodium (mg):	829	Fat:	1.5
Protein (gm):	16		
Carbohydrate (gm):	63.7		

ARTICHOKE AND OLIVE PIZZA

Although olives are high in fat, a few go a long way in this flavorful pizza topping. For the crust, use our Basic Pizza Crust on page 156, a pre-made pizza shell, or dough from the dairy case.

4 Servings

- 3/4 cup canned artichoke hearts, drained
- 1 medium-sized onion, chopped
- 1 large garlic clove, minced
- 3/4 cup reduced-fat, reduced-sodium pizza sauce, *or* regular pizza sauce
- 1 Basic Pizza Crust (page 156)
- 8 medium-sized pimiento-stuffed green olives, sliced
- 1/2 oz. (2 tablespoons) grated Parmesan cheese
- 2 ozs. (1/2 cup loosely packed) shredded reduced-fat mozzarella cheese

1. Preheat oven to 450 degrees. Remove and discard coarse outer leaves from artichoke hearts. Coarsely chop hearts. Reserve.

2. In a 1-cup measure, combine onions and garlic. Cover with wax paper, and microwave on high power 2 minutes or until onions are softened.

3. Meanwhile, form pizza crust (if homemade). Spread sauce evenly over crust, leaving a 1/4-inch border uncovered at outer edge. Spoon onions and garlic mixture evenly over sauce. Add artichokes and olives, distributing them evenly. Sprinkle evenly with Parmesan, then mozzarella.

4. Bake in preheated oven 15 to 17 minutes (or according to directions if a purchased crust is used) or until edges of crust are browned. Cut into 8 wedges or rectangles.

Nutritional Data

PER SERVING		EXCHANGES	
Calories:	318	Milk:	0.0
% Calories from fat:	18	Vegetable:	2.0
Fat (gm):	6.5	Fruit:	0.0
Sat. fat (gm):	1.4	Bread:	3.0
Cholesterol (mg):	2.5	Meat:	0.0
Sodium (mg):	662	Fat:	1.0
Protein (gm):	10.7		
Carbohydrate (gm):	55.3		

PEPPERONI PIZZA

Pepperoni sausage is a very high fat ingredient, which must be used judiciously in healthful recipes. However, when it is diced and incorporated into a sauce, a little will go a long way.

4 Servings

- 2 ozs. pepperoni, diced
- 1 medium-sized onion, chopped
- 1 large garlic clove, minced
- 1 cup reduced-sodium tomato sauce, *or* regular tomato sauce
- 1 teaspoon Italian seasoning
- ⅛ teaspoon salt (optional)
- ⅛ teaspoon black pepper
- 1 Basic Pizza Crust (page 156), *or* purchased crust
- 3 ozs. (¾ cup loosely packed) shredded reduced-fat mozzarella cheese

1. Preheat oven to 425 degrees. In a 10-inch nonstick skillet, combine pepperoni, onions, and garlic. Cook over medium heat, stirring frequently, until onions are tender, 5 to 6 minutes. Turn out onto a plate lined with paper towels to blot up excess fat.

2. Return mixture to skillet. Stir in tomato sauce, Italian seasoning, salt, if desired, and black pepper. Stir to mix. Cook over medium heat, stirring frequently, 2 minutes longer.

3. Form pizza crust (if homemade). Spread sauce evenly over crust, leaving a ¼-inch border uncovered at outer edge. Sprinkle evenly with cheese.

4. Bake in preheated oven 15 to 17 minutes (or according to directions if a purchased crust is used) or until edges of crust are browned. Cut into 8 wedges or rectangles.

Nutritional Data

PER SERVING		EXCHANGES	
Calories:	393	Milk:	0.0
% Calories from fat:	29	Vegetable:	2.0
Fat (gm):	12.8	Fruit:	0.0
Sat. fat (gm):	3.6	Bread:	3.0
Cholesterol (mg):	0	Meat:	0.5
Sodium (mg):	720	Fat:	2.0
Protein (gm):	13.2		
Carbohydrate (gm):	55.9		

CALZONE DOUGH

Use this easy dough for either of the calzone recipes that follow. Preparation is quick and easy when you make the dough in the food processor and use rapid-rising yeast.

6 Servings

2¾–3 cups all-purpose white flour
  1 package rapid-rising yeast
  ½ teaspoon salt
  ½ teaspoon sugar
  1 cup (scant) hot water (125–130 degrees)
  1 tablespoon olive oil

1. In a food processor container fitted with a steel blade, combine 2¾ cups flour, yeast, salt, and sugar. Pulse to mix.

2. Combine water and oil in a saucepan. Heat mixture over medium-high heat to 125 degrees (or until it feels hot but does not burn fingertips). With food processor on, gradually add water-oil mixture through feed tube. Process until dough forms a mass, 5 to 10 seconds. Process 1 minute longer to knead. If necessary, add additional flour through feed tube, and continue processing until dough cleans sides of bowl. Remove dough from processor.

3. Turn dough out onto a lightly floured board. Cover with plastic wrap coated with nonstick spray, and let rise in a warm place 15 minutes. Preheat oven to 375 degrees.

4. Divide dough into 6 equal pieces. On a lightly floured board, roll each portion of dough into a 7-inch circle, adding additional flour to board if needed. (Hint: if dough is difficult to roll to this diameter, roll each circle to 6 inches; then allow dough to rest before rolling out to 7 inches.) Stack circles on a plate, covering with cooking-spray-coated plastic wrap. Refrigerate until needed.

Nutritional Data

PER SERVING		EXCHANGES	
Calories:	233	Milk:	0.0
% Calories from fat:	11	Vegetable:	0.0
Fat (gm):	2.8	Fruit:	0.0
Sat. fat (gm):	0.4	Bread:	3.0
Cholesterol (mg):	0	Meat:	0.0
Sodium (mg):	179	Fat:	0.5
Protein (gm):	6.4		
Carbohydrate (gm):	44.6		

Spinach Calzone

*Here's an appealing spinach and cheese filling for calzone.
Softening the onions in the microwave eliminates extra
fat and speeds preparation.*

6 Servings

- 1 recipe Calzone Dough (page 162)
  Cornmeal for baking sheets (optional)
- 1 medium-sized onion, chopped
- 1 cup nonfat ricotta cheese
- 1½ cups (6 ozs.) shredded reduced-fat mozzarella cheese
- ⅓ cup (1½ ozs.) grated nonfat Parmesan cheese topping
- 2 teaspoons olive oil
- 1½ teaspoons Italian seasoning
- 1 garlic clove, minced
  Dash ground nutmeg
- ¼ teaspoon salt (optional)
- 3–4 drops hot pepper sauce
- 1 10-oz. package chopped frozen spinach, thawed and well drained
- 1–2 tablespoons 1% fat milk (optional)

1. Prepare dough according to directions in recipe (page 162). Preheat oven to 375 degrees. Coat 2 large baking sheets with cooking spray. Lightly sprinkle with cornmeal, if desired. Set aside.

2. Place onions in a small microwave-proof bowl, cover with wax paper, and microwave on high power 1½ to 2 minutes.

3. In a large bowl, stir together microwaved onions, ricotta, mozzarella, Parmesan, olive oil, Italian seasoning, garlic, nutmeg, salt, if desired, and hot pepper sauce. A handful at a time, squeeze out as much water from the spinach as possible. Stir spinach into cheese mixture.

4. For each calzone, spoon about ½ cup of filling mixture onto half of one dough circle, leaving ½ inch uncoated at edge. Moisten edges of dough with water. Fold dough in half over filling. Seal by pressing with fork tines.

5. Transfer calzone to prepared baking sheets. Prick tops to allow steam to escape. For more attractive browning, brush tops of calzone lightly with milk before baking. Bake 20 to 25 minutes on center oven rack or

until crust is lightly browned. If sheets must be baked on two racks, reverse their positions halfway through baking. Allow calzone to cool 3 or 4 minutes before serving.

Nutritional Data

PER SERVING		EXCHANGES	
Calories:	374	Milk:	0.0
% Calories from fat:	19	Vegetable:	2.5
Fat (gm):	7.9	Fruit:	0.0
Sat. fat (gm):	1.7	Bread:	3.0
Cholesterol (mg):	0	Meat:	1.0
Sodium (mg):	461	Fat:	1.0
Protein (gm):	18.1		
Carbohydrate (gm):	59.4		

SAUSAGE AND PEPPERS CALZONE

Italian-style turkey sausage, which is lower in fat than regular sausage, works very well in this tasty calzone filling. Bulk sausage is most convenient, but links can be used. For the dough, see our recipe on page 162.

6 Servings

- 1 recipe Calzone Dough (page 162)
  Cornmeal for baking sheets (optional)
- 6 ozs. Italian-style turkey sausage
- 1 16-oz. bag frozen mixed red, green, and yellow peppers and onions
- 1 8-oz. can reduced-sodium tomato sauce, *or* regular tomato sauce
- 1 cup sliced mushrooms
- 1 teaspoon olive oil
- 2 garlic cloves, minced
- 1½ teaspoons Italian seasoning
- ¼ teaspoon salt (optional)
- ⅛ teaspoon black pepper
- 1–2 tablespoons 1% fat milk (optional)

1. Prepare dough according to directions in recipe. Preheat oven to 375 degrees. Coat 2 large baking sheets with cooking spray. Lightly sprinkle with cornmeal, if desired. Set aside.

2. If sausage has casing, remove and discard. Cut or break sausage into small pieces. In a 12-inch nonstick skillet, cook sausage over medium heat, breaking up large pieces, until it changes color and is cooked through. Turn sausage out onto paper towels to blot fat.

3. Coarsely chop any large pieces of onions in peppers-onions mixture. Return sausage to skillet. Add peppers and onions, tomato sauce, mushrooms, oil, garlic, Italian seasoning, salt, if desired, and black pepper. Cook, uncovered, over medium heat, stirring frequently, until peppers are tender and sauce has cooked down somewhat, 13 to 16 minutes.

4. For each calzone, spoon about ½ cup of filling mixture onto half of one dough circle, leaving ½-inch uncoated at edge. Moisten edges of dough with water. Fold dough in half over filling. Seal by pressing edges with fork tines.

5. Transfer calzone to prepared baking sheets. Prick tops to allow steam to escape. For more attractive browning, brush tops of calzone lightly with milk before baking. Bake on center oven rack 20 to 25 minutes or until crust is lightly browned. If sheets must be baked on two racks, reverse their positions halfway through baking. Allow calzone to cool 3 or 4 minutes before serving.

Nutritional Data

PER SERVING		EXCHANGES	
Calories:	345	Milk:	0.0
% Calories from fat:	23	Vegetable:	2.0
Fat (gm):	8.8	Fruit:	0.0
Sat. fat (gm):	1.3	Bread:	3.0
Cholesterol (mg):	22.9	Meat:	0.5
Sodium (mg):	388	Fat:	1.0
Protein (gm):	12.6		
Carbohydrate (gm):	53.9		

FOCACCIA WITH ONIONS AND SUN-DRIED TOMATOES

Focaccia is a trendy addition to many bakery and restaurant menus. But it's easy and fun to make at home. The bread tastes best the day it's made. Freeze it for longer storage.

If you have a heavy-duty mixer equipped with a bread hook, use it to knead the dough; otherwise knead by hand.

15 Servings

³/₄ cup dry-packed sun-dried tomatoes
3¹/₂–4¹/₄ cups all-purpose white flour, divided
¹/₂ cup finely chopped onions
2 garlic cloves, minced
1 tablespoon olive oil, preferably extra-virgin
1 teaspoon dried rosemary, crushed
1 teaspoon sugar
³/₄ teaspoon salt
1 packet rapid-rising dry yeast
1¹/₄ cups hot water (125 to 130 degrees)
3–4 drops hot pepper sauce

Glaze
1 tablespoon olive oil, preferably extra-virgin
1 tablespoon tomato paste
1 teaspoon dried rosemary, crushed

1. Coat a 9¹/₂-in. x 13-in. pan with cooking spray and set aside. In a cup or small bowl, cover sun-dried tomatoes with hot water. Let stand 5 or 10 minutes to soften. Drain well. Chop and set aside.

2. In a large mixing bowl, combine 2 cups of flour, onions, garlic, reserved tomatoes, oil, rosemary, sugar, salt, and yeast.

3. In a saucepan, heat water over medium-high heat to 125 degrees (or until it feels hot but does not burn fingertips). Add water and hot pepper sauce to other ingredients. Beat with an electric mixer on low speed for 1 minute, scraping bowl frequently. Raise speed to medium and beat 1 minute, scraping bowl frequently. Adding ³/₄ cup flour at a time, stir in enough remaining flour to make dough easy to handle. Form into a ball.

4. Use mixer dough hook to knead dough 8 to 9 minutes until very cohesive and elastic. Alternatively, turn out onto a lightly floured board, and knead with hands 9 to 10 minutes until very cohesive. Transfer dough to prepared pan. Press and spread dough to cover bottom surface of pan, making thickness even. Cover with cooking-spray-coated plastic wrap and allow to rise in a warm place 40 to 45 minutes, until dough has risen about one-half inch. Press random indentations into dough with your knuckle to create an uneven surface. Preheat oven to 400 degrees.

5. *For glaze:* Mix together oil, tomato paste, and rosemary. Set aside.

6. Bake bread 20 minutes. Remove from oven and brush surface of bread lightly with glaze. Appearance will be streaked. Return to oven and bake an additional 15 to 20 minutes until lightly browned on top. Remove bread from pan. Cool on a wire rack. Cut into rectangles.

Nutritional Data

PER SERVING		EXCHANGES	
Calories:	136	Milk:	0.0
% Calories from fat:	15	Vegetable:	0.0
Fat (gm):	2.2	Fruit:	0.0
Sat. fat (gm):	0.3	Bread:	1.5
Cholesterol (mg):	0	Meat:	0.0
Sodium (mg):	173	Fat:	0.5
Protein (gm):	3.7		
Carbohydrate (gm):	25.1		

SESAME BREADSTICKS

◆

*These go well with any of the hearty, warming soups
in this book. They also make a nice snack or tempting
accompaniment to a luncheon salad.*

*Since the dough is prepared in a food processor,
mixing and kneading are fast and easy.*

Makes 12 breadsticks

2¹⁄₃–2³⁄₄ cups all-purpose white flour, divided
1 packet rapid-rising dry yeast
1 cup water
1¹⁄₂ tablespoons extra-virgin olive oil, divided
³⁄₄ teaspoon salt
3 tablespoons sesame seeds
  Sea salt, kosher salt, *or* other coarse salt, for
  garnish (optional)

1. Combine 1¹⁄₃ cups white flour and yeast in a food processor fitted with a steel blade. Pulse several times to mix well. Combine water, 1 tablespoon oil, and salt in a saucepan. Stirring until salt dissolves, heat mixture over medium-high heat to 125 degrees (or until it feels hot but does not burn fingertips).

2. With processor running, pour liquid through feed tube into flour until all liquid has been added. Process 1¹⁄₂ minutes. Add 1 cup more flour. If dough does not form a firm ball that cleans the bowl sides when flour is fully incorporated, gradually add more flour through feed tube until it reaches that point.

3. Lightly brush ball of dough with a small amount of remaining oil. Place in a medium-sized bowl. Tightly cover bowl with plastic wrap. Set aside in a warm place until dough doubles in bulk, about 45 minutes. Meanwhile, coat two large baking sheets with cooking spray. Preheat oven to 425 degrees.

4. Punch down dough; knead briefly. On a cutting board, shape dough into an 8-inch evenly thick log. Cut log into quarters. Then cut each quarter into 3 equal pieces. Grasping each end of piece with hands, stretch out. Then roll back and forth to form a 10-inch stick. Place sticks on baking sheets, spacing them about 2 inches apart. Brush sticks lightly with remaining olive oil. Sprinkle with sesame seeds and coarse salt, if desired.

5. Bake one pan at a time in upper third of oven 11 to 14 minutes or until sticks are lightly browned and slightly puffed. Transfer pan to cooling rack; let stand 5 minutes and serve.

Nutritional Data

PER BREADSTICK		EXCHANGES	
Calories:	117	Milk:	0.0
% Calories from fat:	23	Vegetable:	0.0
Fat (gm):	3	Fruit:	0.0
Sat. fat (gm):	0.4	Bread:	1.0
Cholesterol (mg):	0	Meat:	0.0
Sodium (mg):	135	Fat:	1.0
Protein (gm):	3.3		
Carbohydrate (gm):	19		

11
DESSERTS

Zuppa Inglese

Tiramisu

Almond Biscotti

Chocolate-Hazelnut Biscotti

Chocolate-Meringue Cookies

Ricotta Cheesecake

Pear-Almond Cake

Caramel-Glazed Bread Pudding

Lemon Granita

Poached Peaches

ZUPPA INGLESE

This rich-tasting and festive dessert makes a wonderful finale to a company meal. Although the custard must be prepared ahead, the dish is really quite easy. The recipe suggests using strawberries, blueberries, and peaches. However, you can substitute raspberries, pineapple, and kiwi fruit for an equally colorful one. Or use other seasonal berries and fruits you have on hand.

8 Servings

Custard

      1 large egg white
      1 large egg
   2½ cups 1% fat milk
    ⅓ cup granulated sugar
    ¼ cup cornstarch
      1 tablespoon butter, *or* margarine
   2½ teaspoons vanilla extract

Fruit

      5 cups fresh fruit (a combination of blueberries, hulled and sliced strawberries, and/or peeled and sliced peaches)
    ⅓ cup granulated sugar
      3 tablespoons rum, *or* fruit brandy

To assemble

    10 ozs. non-fat pound cake, *or* angel food cake

1. *For custard:* In a 4-cup glass measure or similar microwave-proof bowl, beat together egg and egg white with a fork or wire whisk until smooth and frothy. Stir in milk. Cover with wax paper, and microwave on high power 2½ to 3½ minutes, stopping and stirring three times, until the mixture is hot but not boiling.

2. In the top of a double boiler, mix together sugar and cornstarch. Gradually beat in heated milk mixture, stirring vigorously and scraping the pan bottom until smooth. Cook over boiling water, stirring vigorously, 6 to 7 minutes or until mixture thickens. Remove from heat. Stir in butter and vanilla. Cover and refrigerate 3 or 4 hours or up to 48 hours.

3. *For fruit:* Combine fruit in a medium bowl. Add sugar and rum. Stir to mix. Cover and refrigerate ½ hour.

4. *To assemble:* If using pound cake, cut into thin slices. If using angel food cake, cut into cubes. In bottom of a large glass bowl with straight sides, arrange one third of cake slices or cubes. Spoon 1/3 of fruit mixture over cake. Top with 1/3 of custard. Repeat layers, reserving 1/3 cup of fruit mixture for garnish. Arrange remaining fruit atop center of dessert. Cover and refrigerate several hours or up to 24 hours.

Nutritional Data

PER SERVING		EXCHANGES	
Calories:	292	Milk:	0.0
% Calories from fat:	10	Vegetable:	0.0
Fat (gm):	3.2	Fruit:	1.0
Sat. fat (gm):	1.6	Bread:	3.0
Cholesterol (mg):	33.6	Meat:	0.0
Sodium (mg):	207	Fat:	0.5
Protein (gm):	5.6		
Carbohydrate (gm):	58.9		

TIRAMISU

*There are scores of recipes for tiramisu. In most classic
recipes, the filling is made with marscapone cheese, which is
astronomically high in fat, and raw eggs, which are now
considered too risky to eat. We took an entirely different approach
and experimented with ingredients that would retain much of the
classic flavor while cutting the fat and omitting uncooked eggs.
Not only is this version better for you, it's quick and easy.*

8 Servings

1 1/4 cups freshly made espresso, *or* use instant
 espresso granules
1–2 tablespoons rum (optional)
1 1/2 cups reduced-fat cottage cheese (1% fat)
 1/4 cup water
 1 7-oz. jar marshmallow cream
 1/2 teaspoon almond extract
 4 ozs. Neufchâtel cheese, cut into 4 chunks
 4 ozs. nonfat cream cheese, cut into 4 chunks
 9 ozs. ladyfingers
 1 oz. top-quality semisweet, *or* bittersweet,
 chocolate (not unsweetened), grated or very
 finely chopped

1. Combine espresso and rum, if desired, and set aside to cool slightly.

2. Meanwhile, in a food processor container, combine cottage cheese and
 water. Process 1 minute or until cottage cheese is almost smooth. Add
 marshmallow cream and almond extract, and process 20 seconds to
 incorporate. With processor running, add chunks of Neufchâtel and
 cream cheese one at a time through feed tube. Process until smooth
 and cream cheese is completely incorporated.

3. Arrange half of ladyfingers in a 2-quart flat glass baking dish. Carefully,
 spoon 1/2 of espresso mixture over ladyfingers. Spoon 1/2 of cheese
 mixture over ladyfingers, spreading evenly. Sprinkle evenly with half of
 grated chocolate. Lay remaining ladyfingers over first layer. Spoon
 over remaining coffee mixture, being very careful not to drip any onto
 the sauce below. Spoon remaining cheese mixture over ladyfingers.
 Finish by sprinkling remaining chocolate evenly over top layer.

4. Insert 6 to 8 toothpicks into top of tiramisu to keep plastic wrap from touching sauce. Cover with plastic wrap and refrigerate until completely chilled and flavors are well blended, 6 hours or up to 24 hours.

Nutritional Data

PER SERVING		EXCHANGES	
Calories:	293	Milk:	0.0
% Calories from fat:	24	Vegetable:	0.0
Fat (gm):	7.9	Fruit:	0.0
Sat. fat (gm):	4	Bread:	3.0
Cholesterol (mg):	129.1	Meat:	0.5
Sodium (mg):	373	Fat:	1.0
Protein (gm):	12.8		
Carbohydrate (gm):	43.2		

ALMOND BISCOTTI

Mild and crunchy crisp, these are great dunking cookies to serve with cappuccino.

Makes 35–40 biscotti

1/2 cup chopped blanched slivered almonds, divided
1 cup granulated sugar
1 large egg
2 large egg whites
1 tablespoon lemon juice
Pinch of very finely grated lemon zest (yellow part of peel), *or* 3 drops of lemon extract
1 teaspoon almond extract
2 2/3 cups all-purpose white flour
1 teaspoon baking powder
1/4 teaspoon baking soda
1/8 teaspoon salt

1. Preheat oven to 350 degrees. Coat a 12-in. x 18-in. or similar very large baking sheet with cooking spray; set aside.

2. Spread almonds in a baking dish and toast, stirring several times, 6 to 8 minutes, until tinged with brown. Remove from oven; let stand until cooled.

3. Combine 1/3 cup toasted almonds and sugar in a food processor bowl. (Reserve remaining nuts for adding later.) Process continuously for several minutes or until almonds are ground to a crumbly meal. Add egg and whites, lemon juice and zest, and almond extract. Process until smoothly blended.

4. In a medium-sized bowl, thoroughly stir together flour, baking powder, baking soda, and salt. Turn out processed mixture into flour mixture. Add remaining chopped toasted almonds. Stir until mixed, using a large wooden spoon. Then knead lightly with hands to form a smooth, cohesive dough.

5. Divide dough in half. With lightly oiled hands, shape each half into a smooth, evenly shaped 2-inch-wide by 12-inch-long log. Smooth surface by rolling each log back and forth on a clean work surface. Transfer logs to baking sheet, spacing at least 3 inches apart. Press down on logs to flatten slightly.

6. Bake logs 25 minutes; their surface may crack. Remove pan from oven. Gently slide logs onto a cutting board. Using a serrated knife and working carefully, cut logs diagonally into ³/₈-inch-thick slices. (If they seem crumbly, let cool a few minutes before slicing.)

7. Lay slices flat on baking sheet. Return to oven. Toast 15 to 20 minutes, turning over slices halfway through, until they are just tinged with brown. (The longer the baking time, the crunchier and drier the slices.) Transfer slices to racks; let stand until completely cooled. You can store airtight for up to 10 days. Freeze for longer storage.

Nutritional Data

PER BISCOTTO		EXCHANGES	
Calories:	70	Milk:	0.0
% Calories from fat:	14	Vegetable:	0.0
Fat (gm):	1.1	Fruit:	0.0
Sat. fat (gm):	0.1	Bread:	1.0
Cholesterol (mg):	6.1	Meat:	0.0
Sodium (mg):	31	Fat:	0.0
Protein (gm):	1.7		
Carbohydrate (gm):	13.4		

CHOCOLATE-HAZELNUT BISCOTTI

These crunchy-crisp cookies are good plain, but they may be dressed up with a drizzle of chocolate glaze, if desired.

Makes about 35–40 biscotti

- 1/2 cup whole hazelnuts, divided
- 1 cup granulated sugar
- 2 large eggs
- 2 large egg whites
- 1 tablespoon water
- 3/4 teaspoon almond extract
- 2 1/2 cups all-purpose white flour
- 1/4 cup European-style (Dutch-process) cocoa powder
- 1 1/4 teaspoons baking powder
- 1/8 teaspoon salt

Optional Glaze

- 1 oz. semisweet chocolate, chopped
- 1/4 teaspoon light corn syrup

1. Preheat oven to 350 degrees. Grease a 12-in. x 15-in. or larger baking sheet; set aside.

2. Spread hazelnuts in a baking dish. Toast, stirring several times, 8 to 11 minutes or until hulls loosen and nuts are tinged with brown. Remove from oven and let stand until cooled. Remove any loose bits of hull by rubbing nuts between hands or in a tea towel. Coarsely chop hazelnuts.

3. Combine 1/3 cup chopped hazelnuts and sugar in a food processor bowl. (Reserve remaining nuts for adding later.) Process continuously for several minutes or until nuts are ground to a crumbly meal. Add eggs and whites, water, and almond extract. Process until smoothly blended.

4. Sift flour, cocoa, baking powder, and salt into a medium-sized bowl. Turn out processed mixture into flour mixture. Add reserved chopped nuts. Stir until mixed, using a large wooden spoon. Lightly knead mixture until it holds together smoothly.

5. Divide dough in half. With lightly oiled hands, shape each half into a smooth, evenly shaped 1½-inch-wide by 12-inch-long log. Smooth surface by rolling logs back and forth on a clean work surface. Transfer logs to baking sheet, spacing at least 3 inches apart. Press down on logs to flatten slightly.

6. Bake logs 25 minutes; they may develop cracks. Remove pan from oven. Gently slide logs onto a cutting board. Using a serrated knife and working carefully, cut logs diagonally into ½-inch-thick slices. (If they seem crumbly, let cool a few minutes before slicing.)

7. Lay slices flat on baking sheet and return to oven. Toast 17 to 22 minutes, turning slices about halfway through. (The longer the baking time, the crunchier and drier the slices.) Transfer slices to racks; let stand until completely cooled.

8. *For optional glaze:* In a small microwave-proof bowl, microwave chocolate at half power 1½ to 2 minutes, stopping and stirring every 30 seconds, until melted. Stir in corn syrup until smoothly incorporated. Spoon chocolate into a piping cone or a small plastic baggie. (If using a baggie, press chocolate into one corner and cut away tip to form a tiny hole.) Pipe (or squeeze from baggie) a very fine zigzag line of chocolate back and forth over cooled biscotti. Let stand until chocolate sets, about 2 hours. You can store airtight for up to 10 days. Freeze for longer storage.

Nutritional Data

PER BISCOTTO		EXCHANGES	
Calories:	74	Milk:	0.0
% Calories from fat:	20	Vegetable:	0.0
Fat (gm):	1.7	Fruit:	0.0
Sat. fat (gm):	0.3	Bread:	1.0
Cholesterol (mg):	12.2	Meat:	0.0
Sodium (mg):	27	Fat:	0.0
Protein (gm):	1.9		
Carbohydrate (gm):	13.3		

CHOCOLATE-MERINGUE COOKIES

The meringue in these sweet, crisp-chewy cookies may gradually deflate upon standing, so be sure to form the cookies as soon as the batter is whipped. Also, use two baking sheets large enough to hold all the cookies at once, and then bake both pans (staggered on two oven racks) at the same time.

Makes 40–45 cookies

1/4 cup unsweetened European-style cocoa powder
1 oz. unsweetened chocolate, chopped
1/4 cup cornstarch
1/2 cup powdered sugar
4 large egg whites, at room temperature, completely free of yolk
1/4 teaspoon cream of tartar
Pinch (generous) of salt
1 cup granulated sugar
1/2 teaspoon instant coffee granules
1 1/2 teaspoons vanilla extract

1. Preheat oven to 250 degrees. Line two 12-in. x 18-in. or other very large baking sheets with baking parchment.

2. Combine cocoa powder and chocolate in a food processor bowl. Process until chocolate is finely ground. In a medium-sized bowl thoroughly stir together chocolate mixture, cornstarch, and powdered sugar.

3. In a completely grease-free large mixer bowl, with mixer on high speed, beat egg whites until frothy and opaque. Add cream of tartar and salt; beat whites until soft peaks just begin to form. A bit at a time, add sugar, then coffee granules and vanilla. Scraping down bowl sides several times, continue to beat until mixture stands in stiff, glossy peaks. Using a rubber spatula, quickly fold chocolate mixture into whites until evenly incorporated.

4. Immediately drop batter by tablespoonfuls onto baking sheets, spacing about 1 1/2 inches apart. Transfer pans to oven, staggering them on two racks in center half of oven.

5. Bake 50 to 60 minutes or until cookies are firm on top, exchanging pans halfway through baking to ensure even doneness. (Shorter baking time yields chewier cookies, longer time crisper ones.) With cookies still attached to parchment, place on wire racks until thoroughly cooled. Carefully peel cookies from parchment. You can store cookies airtight for 3 or 4 days. Freeze for longer storage.

Nutritional Data

PER COOKIE		EXCHANGES	
Calories:	35	Milk:	0.0
% Calories from fat:	10	Vegetable:	0.0
Fat (gm):	0.4	Fruit:	0.0
Sat. fat (gm):	0.2	Bread:	0.5
Cholesterol (mg):	0	Meat:	0.0
Sodium (mg):	6	Fat:	0.0
Protein (gm):	0.5		
Carbohydrate (gm):	7.9		

RICOTTA CHEESECAKE

*Ricotta cheesecake has a firmer texture than New York style.
But it's equally flavorful. This version tastes rich without
being high in fat. Serve plain or with fresh fruit. For the
crust, you can use our Almond Biscotti recipe (page 176)
or purchased cookies. Break cookies into small pieces.
Then process to fine crumbs with a food processor.*

10 Servings

- ³/₄ cup biscotti crumbs, made from low-fat biscotti
- 1 15-oz. carton part-skim ricotta cheese
- 1 cup nonfat ricotta cheese
- ¹/₂ cup granulated sugar
- ¹/₂ cup liquid egg substitute
- ¹/₃ cup all-purpose white flour
- 1 tablespoon vanilla extract
  Grated zest (yellow part of peel) from ¹/₂ lemon
- 1 8-oz. package nonfat cream cheese, cut into 10 chunks
- ¹/₂ cup golden raisins
- 1¹/₂ cups sliced large strawberries, *or* other fruit for garnish (optional)

1. Adjust oven rack to center of oven, and preheat to 350 degrees. Spread biscotti crumbs in a 9-inch nonstick springform pan lightly coated with cooking spray. In a food processor container, combine ricotta cheeses, sugar, egg substitute, flour, vanilla, and lemon zest. Process 1 minute until smooth. Through feed tube, add chunks of cream cheese one at a time. Blend until smooth. Turn off processor. Stir in raisins.

2. Carefully spoon cheese mixture over crumb base, being careful not to disturb crumbs. Spread ricotta mixture out evenly with the back of a large spoon. Place springform pan on a baking sheet, and bake 45 to 50 minutes in preheated oven until center of cake appears nearly set when shaken. Turn off oven. Leave cake in oven with door closed for an additional 20 minutes.

3. Cool on a wire rack 20 minutes. Loosen sides of cake by running a knife around inside edge of the pan. Remove springform. Refrigerate cake 3 or 4 hours or up to 48 hours before serving.

4. When cake has cooled, store covered with plastic wrap in refrigerator. Before serving, decorate outside edge of top with a ring of strawberry slices or other fruit, if desired.

Nutritional Data

PER SERVING		EXCHANGES	
Calories:	197	Milk:	0.0
% Calories from fat:	13	Vegetable:	0.0
Fat (gm):	2.8	Fruit:	0.5
Sat. fat (gm):	0.3	Bread:	1.5
Cholesterol (mg):	6	Meat:	1.0
Sodium (mg):	247	Fat:	0.0
Protein (gm):	12.5		
Carbohydrate (gm):	30.3		

PEAR-ALMOND CAKE

◆

*The flavors of pears and almonds go together beautifully
in this homey, succulent cake. It is best served fresh, as the pears
gradually exude their juice and cause the cake to become soggy.*

7 Servings

- 4 large peeled and cored ripe pears, cut into chunks and tossed with 2 teaspoons fresh lemon juice
- 2 tablespoons plus ⅔ cup granulated sugar, divided
- 1⅔ cups all-purpose white flour
- 1¼ teaspoons baking powder
- ¼ teaspoon baking soda
- ¼ teaspoon salt
- ¼ teaspoon ground ginger
- 2 tablespoons butter, *or* non-diet, tub-style margarine, slightly softened
- 1 tablespoon canola oil
- 1 large egg
- 2 teaspoons vanilla extract
- ¾ teaspoon finely grated lemon zest (yellow part of peel)
- ¾ teaspoon almond extract
- ⅔ cup skim milk
- 2 tablespoons sliced unblanched almonds, for garnish (optional)

1. Preheat oven to 500 degrees. Generously coat a medium-sized, rimmed baking sheet with cooking spray. Coat a 9-inch (or similar) springform pan with cooking spray.

2. Spread pears on baking sheet. Sprinkle with 2 tablespoons sugar. Bake in upper third of oven, stirring once or twice, 7 to 10 minutes or until pears are bubbly and beginning to brown. Remove from oven; let cool slightly. *Reset oven to 375 degrees.*

3. Thoroughly stir together flour, baking powder, baking soda, salt, and ginger in a medium-sized bowl.

4. In a mixing bowl with mixer on medium speed, beat remaining ⅔ cup sugar, butter, and oil until light and well blended. Beat in egg, vanilla, lemon zest, and almond extract. Gently fold in half of dry ingredients. Lightly stir in milk, then remainder of dry ingredients just until thor-

oughly incorporated but not over-mixed. Immediately spread generous half of batter evenly in springform pan. Top with pears, sprinkling evenly over batter. Cover with remaining batter. Sprinkle with almonds, if desired.

5. Bake cake in center third of oven 25 to 30 minutes or until a toothpick inserted in cake center comes out clean. Let cool on wire rack. Serve warm or at room temperature.

Nutritional Data

PER SERVING		EXCHANGES	
Calories:	323	Milk:	0.0
% Calories from fat:	18	Vegetable:	0.0
Fat (gm):	6.6	Fruit:	1.0
Sat. fat (gm):	2.5	Bread:	3.0
Cholesterol (mg):	39.6	Meat:	0.0
Sodium (mg):	235	Fat:	1.0
Protein (gm):	5.2		
Carbohydrate (gm):	61.7		

CARAMEL-GLAZED BREAD PUDDING

This is really a cross between a caramel flan and a bread pudding. It is best served at room temperature or just slightly warm.

7 Servings

Caramel Glaze

$^{1}/_{2}$ cup granulated sugar
2$^{1}/_{2}$ tablespoons water
$^{1}/_{2}$ teaspoon light corn syrup

Pudding

2$^{1}/_{2}$ cups $^{1}/_{4}$-in. cubes day-old crustless Italian bread
$^{1}/_{2}$ cup dark seedless raisins
$^{1}/_{3}$ cup light, *or* dark, rum
1 12-oz. can skim evaporated milk
1 cup 2% fat milk
2 tablespoons plus 1 teaspoon all-purpose white flour, divided
6 tablespoons granulated sugar
$^{1}/_{8}$ teaspoon salt
2 large eggs plus 2 large egg whites
2$^{1}/_{2}$ teaspoons vanilla extract
$^{1}/_{8}$ teaspoon finely grated orange zest (orange part of peel)
$^{1}/_{2}$ teaspoon almond extract

1. Preheat oven to 350 degrees. Set out a 6- or 7-cup oven-proof mold or round casserole.

2. *For caramel glaze:* Combine sugar, water, and corn syrup in a 2-cup microwave-proof glass measure. Cover with wax paper. Microwave on high power until mixture comes to a boil, 1$^{1}/_{2}$ to 2 minutes. Boil 1 minute; then stop and stir mixture using a clean, dry spoon. Uncover and continue microwaving on high power until mixture turns a very pale amber color, 1 to 1$^{1}/_{2}$ minutes longer; watch closely as mixture will color and then become too dark very rapidly.

3. Using a kitchen mitt or hot pad, immediately remove glaze from microwave oven. *Working carefully as mixture is extremely hot,*

immediately pour into mold, slowly tipping it from side to side to coat as much of the bottom and sides as possible. (If using a metal mold, hold it with kitchen mitts, as it will become very hot.) Set aside mold so caramel glaze can cool and firm.

4. *For pudding:* Place bread in a large bowl. Combine raisins and rum in a small microwave-proof bowl. Cover with wax paper, and microwave on high power 1 minute; set aside.

5. Combine evaporated milk and 2% milk in a 4-cup glass measure. Microwave on high power 3 to 4 minutes, stopping and stirring at 1-minute intervals until mixture is very hot but not boiling. Pour mixture over bread. Let stand until mixture cools to lukewarm.

6. In a small, deep bowl stir together 2 tablespoons flour, granulated sugar, and salt. Using a fork, beat in eggs and whites, vanilla, orange zest, and almond extract until smoothly incorporated.

7. Using a fork, beat bread-milk mixture until it forms a mush. A bit at a time, beat bread-milk mixture and any unabsorbed rum from raisins into egg mixture until well blended. Turn out mixture into caramel-glazed mold.

8. Pat reserved raisins dry on paper towels. Sprinkle them with remaining teaspoon of flour. Sprinkle raisins over pudding; lightly fold them into pudding using a knife blade.

9. Bake on center oven rack 25 to 35 minutes or until pudding appears barely set in center when pan is jiggled. Transfer mold to a wire rack. Cool thoroughly. Run a knife around pudding to loosen it. Turn out onto a serving plate. Serve immediately, or cover and refrigerate up to 48 hours until needed. Let warm up slightly before serving.

Nutritional Data

PER SERVING		EXCHANGES	
Calories:	279	Milk:	0.5
% Calories from fat:	9	Vegetable:	0.0
Fat (gm):	2.7	Fruit:	0.5
Sat. fat (gm):	1	Bread:	2.5
Cholesterol (mg):	65	Meat:	0.0
Sodium (mg):	203	Fat:	0.5
Protein (gm):	9.1		
Carbohydrate (gm):	48.7		

LEMON GRANITA

*This simple dessert boasts a wonderful lemony tartness
and taste and an icy, slushy consistency. Unlike sherbet,
it does not require an ice cream maker.*

6 Servings (makes a scant quart)

- ²/₃ cup fresh lemon juice
- 2 teaspoons very finely grated lemon zest (yellow part of peel)
- 2³/₄ cups water
- 1 cup granulated sugar
- 1 tablespoon light corn syrup
- Mint leaves, for garnish (optional)

1. Combine juice and zest in a 1-cup glass measure; set aside.

2. Stir together water, sugar, and corn syrup in a medium-sized saucepan. Bring just to a boil over medium-high heat. Cover and gently boil 1½ minutes. Remove lid and continue boiling, without stirring, 2 minutes longer. Remove from heat; let stand until lukewarm. Stir reserved lemon juice mixture into sugar mixture.

3. Pour mixture into a large, shallow, noncorrosive container or bowl. Freeze, covered, at least 4 hours, stirring mixture with a fork several times during freezing to break it up and form icy crystals.

4. Just before serving, let mixture stand 5 minutes at room temperature to soften slightly. Break up and fluff with a fork again. Serve granita piled into parfait glasses or sherbet dishes. Garnish with mint leaves, if desired. Store in freezer (tightly covered) up to 4 days.

Nutritional Data

PER SERVING		EXCHANGES	
Calories:	146	Milk:	0.0
% Calories from fat:	0	Vegetable:	0.0
Fat (gm):	0	Fruit:	0.0
Sat. fat (gm):	0	Bread:	2.0
Cholesterol (mg):	0	Meat:	0.0
Sodium (mg):	3	Fat:	0.0
Protein (gm):	0.1		
Carbohydrate (gm):	38.3		

POACHED PEACHES

◆

Italians often enjoy fresh or poached fruit for dessert, and since it is virtually fat-free, it's a good choice even if you're not Italian!

Poached peaches may be served in their own cooking liquid or, for a more dramatic and colorful presentation, drizzled with an easy raspberry sauce.

4 Servings

1⅓ cups water
⅓ cup granulated sugar
¼ cup dry white wine, *or* orange juice
4 medium-sized ripe peaches, peeled, halved, and pitted
1 2-in. x 1-in. piece lemon zest (yellow part of peel)
1 2-in.–3-in. piece vanilla bean, *or* ½ teaspoon vanilla extract

Optional Raspberry Sauce

1 10-oz. package frozen raspberries in syrup, thawed

1. In a large saucepan, bring water and sugar to a boil over high heat, stirring until sugar dissolves. Stir in wine. Lower heat so mixture barely simmers. Add peach halves, lemon zest, and vanilla bean (if using vanilla extract, reserve for adding later). Cover and gently simmer peaches until just barely tender, about 5 minutes. Using a slotted spoon, immediately transfer peaches to a medium-sized bowl.

2. Bring syrup to a boil, and briskly simmer about 5 minutes longer until reduced to about 1 cup. Discard lemon zest and vanilla bean (or stir in vanilla extract, if using). Pour syrup over peaches. Refrigerate until chilled, at least 1 hour and up to 3 days. Serve peaches with poaching liquid spooned over top. Or, if serving with raspberry sauce, prepare as follows:

3. *For raspberry sauce:* Press raspberries and their syrup through a fine sieve until pulp is forced through and only seeds remain; discard seeds. Cover and chill sauce. At serving time, remove peaches from poaching syrup using a slotted spoon. Serve with raspberry sauce spooned over top.

Nutritional Data

PER SERVING		EXCHANGES	
Calories:	112	Milk:	0.0
% Calories from fat:	1	Vegetable:	0.0
Fat (gm):	0.1	Fruit:	2.0
Sat. fat (gm):	0	Bread:	0.0
Cholesterol (mg):	0	Meat:	0.0
Sodium (mg):	1	Fat:	0.0
Protein (gm):	0.6		
Carbohydrate (gm):	26.5		

INDEX